CONTENTS

Glossary and Abbreviations	2
Chapter 1: They were the First – The Resurgence of Attack Aviation	3
Chapter 2: In Special Circumstances	10
Chapter 3: 'Two Hundredths' – Second Shift	18
Chapter 4: The Rooks in Bagram	26
Chapter 5: From Squadron to Regiment	35
Chapter 6: 378th Independent Attack Aviation Regiment, 1984–1985	48
Appendix: Attack Aviation as Part of the 40th Army Air Force	69
Notes	70
Bibliography	71

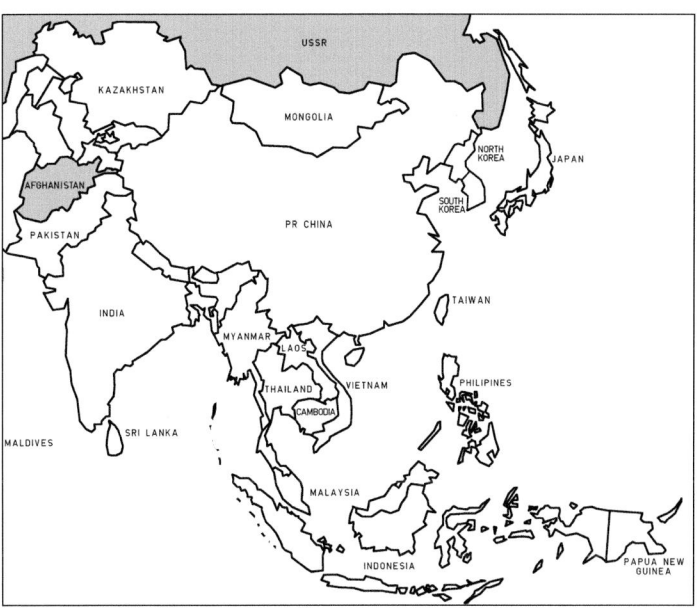

Helion & Company Limited
Unit 8 Amherst Business Centre
Budbrooke Road
Warwick
CV34 5WE
England
Tel. 01926 499 619
Fax 0121 711 4075
Email: info@helion.co.uk
Website: www.helion.co.uk
Twitter: @helionbooks
Visit our blog http://blog.helion.co.uk/

Published by Helion & Company 2023
Designed and typeset by Mach 3 Solutions Ltd (www.mach3solutions.co.uk)
Cover designed by Paul Hewitt, Battlefield Design (www.battlefield-design.co.uk)

Text © Andrey Korotkov 2023
Diagrams and Maps © Tom Cooper 2023
Artworks © Yuriy Tepsurkaev 2023
Photographs were sourced from (including personal archives) the author, S. Aksenov, A. Araslanov, S. Burdin, V. Butorin, Vaitsckauskas, N. Vdovin, V. Vysotsky, V. Goncharenko, S. Gorshkov, S.Gritskevich, E. Derkulsky, A. Ermakov, V. Zinchenko, N. Korovin, A. Kramarevsky, T. Kononenko, Y. Krylov, A. Kudryavtsev, V. Kuzma, V. Leonenkov, N. Lyubimchenko, V. Maksimenko, I. Musyala, S. Moiseev, A. Moseev, I. Neporozhniy, A. Novikov, N. Prikhodko, S. Rodnykh, I. Ryabchenko, S. Salnikov, A. Seregin, V. Simchenko, P. Strizhak, N. Tatarintsev, A. Timofeev, V. Fedchenko, S. Kharchenko, G. Chergizov, B. Chetvertakov, P. Shabalin, Y. Shapurov, S. Shilonosov, V. Yankov, and V. Yatsenko.

ISBN 978-1-804510-13-1

British Library Cataloguing-in-Publication Data.
A catalogue record for this book is available from the British Library.

All rights reserved. No part of this publication may be reproduced, stored in a retrieval system, or transmitted, in any form, or by any means, electronic, mechanical, photocopying, recording or otherwise, without the express written consent of Helion & Company Limited.

For details of other military history titles published by Helion & Company Limited contact the above address, or visit our website: http://www.helion.co.uk.

We always welcome receiving book proposals from prospective authors.

Glossary and abbreviations

AB	Air Base
ADIB	*Aviatsionnaya diviziya istrebiteley-bombardirovshchikov* (Fighter-Bomber Aviation Division)
AKS-74U	Short for Kalashinkov assault rifle with folding stock, model 1974
APA-5D	Mobile power unit on Ural-4320 truck
APIB	*Aviatsionnyy polk istrebiteley-bombardirovshchikov* (Fighter-Bomber Aviation Regiment)
ARZ	*Aviaremontnyy Zavod* (Aircraft Repair Plant)
ASO	*Avtomat Sbrosa Otrazhateley* (Infra-Red Jammer)
ATC	Air Traffic Control
BC	Battle Button
BD	*Boyevyye Deystviya* (Combat Action)
BMP	*Boyevaya Mashina Pekhoty* (Infantry Fighting Vehicle)
BShU	Air Strike (VVS)
CCG	Combat Control Group (VVS)
CM	Council of Ministers (Government of the USSR)
CPSU	Communist Party of the Soviet Union
CRA	Control and Recording Equipment (VVS)
DRA	Democratic Republic of Afghanistan
FBA	Fighter-Bomber Aviation (VVS)
GenStab	General Staff of the Soviet Armed Forces
GNIKI	Scientific Research Institute (VVS)
GRU	*Glavnoye razvedyvatelnoye upravleniye* (Main Intelligence Directorate)
HQ	Headquarters
IAP	*Istrebitel'nyy aviatsionnyy polk* (Fighter Aviation Regiment)
IAS	*Inzhenerno-aviatsionnaya sluzhba* (Aviation Engineering Service)
IBAP	*Istrebitel'no-bombardirovochnayy aviatsionnyy polk* (Fighter-Bomber Aviation Regiment)
KDP	*Kontrolno-Dispetcherskiy Punkt* (Control Tower)
KHAD	*Sluzhba bezopasnosti* Afghanistana (Afghan Security Service)
KMGU	*Konteyner Malogabaritnykh Gruzov Universalnyye* (Universal Container For Small-Sized Freight)
LTE	Tactical Flight Exercises
MANPADS	
MIC	Commission on Military-Industrial Issues (of the MC)
OKSVA	*Ogranichenyy Kontingent Sovietskih Voysk v Afghanistanu* (Limited Contingent of Soviet Troops in Afghanistan)
ORAE	*Otdelnaya aviatsionnaya eskadrilya takticheskoy razvedki* (Independent Tactical Reconnaissance Aviation Squadron)
OShAE	*Otdelnaya shturmovaya aviatsionnaya eskadrilya* (Independent Attack Aviation Squadron)
OShAP	*Otdelnyy shturmovoy aviatsionnyy polk* (Independent Attack Aviation Regiment)
OVE	*otdelnaya vertoletnaya eskadrilya*, (Independent Helicopter Squadron)
PAN	Aircraft spotter
PTU	Parachute-braking unit
PVO	*Voyska Protivoovzdushnoy Oborny* (Air Force and the Air Defence Force)
RUD	Reconnaissance and Strike Action
SAR	Search and Rescue
SSR	Soviet Socialist Republic
TEC	*Tekhniko-ekspluatatsionnaya chast* (Maintenance Department)
TsBP i PLS	*Tsentr Boyevoy Podgotovki i Pereuchivaniya Letnogo Sostava* (Centre for Combat Employment and Retraining of Personnel)
USSR	Union of Soviet Socialist Republics
VATU	*Vozdushnaya armiya* (Air Army)
VDV	*Vozusho-desantnyye voyska* (Airborne Troops)
V-PVO	See PVO
VVAIU	*Vyssheye voyennoye aviatsionnoye inzhenernoye uchilishche* (Higher Military Aviation Engineering School)
VVS	*Voenno-vozdushnye sily* (Soviet Air Force)
ZVENO	Fourship-Formation of Combat Aircraft

CHAPTER 1
THEY WERE THE FIRST – THE RESURGENCE OF ATTACK AVIATION

By the mid-1950s, in light of the reduction of the total number of Soviet Armed Forces, there was a new Soviet military doctrine reflecting a wave of general 'missile euphoria'. Frontline aviation assumed secondary importance with no opportunity for attack aviation to provide close air support or interception. The opinion of the Soviet military and political leadership was that it did not meet the requirements of the era and was ill-suited for modern warfare. The main task of air support to the troops was to be transferred to bomber aviation, the number of which had to be increased. Additionally, part of the tasks had to be carried out with the help of fighters. On the basis of a report by Marshal Zhukov, Minister of Defence of the Union of Soviet Socialist Republics (USSR) describing the current state and prospects of attack aviation, the leaders of the Party and Government of the USSR decided to abolish the attack aviation of the Soviet Air Force.

Under the Ministry of Defence Directive No. 30660 of 29 April 1956, ground attack aviation was disestablished. Numerous highly-decorated attack aviation units, famous in the battles of the Great Patriotic War (Second World War), were disbanded or partially re-formed and transferred to other branches of aviation and even to other branches of the Armed Forces. The mortally outdated Ilyushin Il-10 and Il-10M piston attack aircraft were decommissioned and scrapped en masse. The few Mikoyan i Gurevich MiG-15bis jet fighters which entered service with attack units shortly before their liquidation, were assigned to bomber aviation. A new type of frontline aviation was born in May 1957: the fighter-bomber aviation (FBA).

Flight personnel who had not been made redundant were partially retrained on MiG-15bis aircraft and transferred to the Air Force and the Air Defence Force (*Voyska Protivoovzdushnoy Oborny*, V-PVO or PVO). The mass production of the successor to the 'flying tanks' – the Il-40 jet aircraft – had barely begun and was cancelled, as was all the experimental development work on ground attack aircraft. The task of providing air support to ground troops and naval forces fell on the shoulders of the frontline bomber aviation and the newly formed FBA, which was to replace the Air Force for many years to come.

However, enthusiasts and supporters of attack aircraft did not give up hope of reviving attack aviation in a new guise in the foreseeable future. The rather complicated history of the emergence of the Sukhoi Su-25 is described in detail in monographs and various journals and is beyond the scope of this book. It can only be said that it was a long and arduous journey from the beginning of the initiative group of the general-type team of the Sukhoi Design Bureau under the leadership of O.S. Samoilovich. In August 1968, they developed the conceptual design of a new generation of attack aircraft which was given the designation Su-25 (plant designation T-8). This led to the production plane being delivered to military units in April–May 1981.

Emergence of the Su-25

Despite the fact that the production attack aircraft began to enter service units in 1981, the aircraft produced at the Sukhoi Design Bureau's experimental plant were subjected to trials by specialists from the 8th Scientific Research Institute of Air Force (GNIKI). Aircraft T8-1 and T8-2 with first flights February and December 1975 respectively, had the status of developmental aircraft. The initiative to get the military involved in the trials from the outset was shown by Deputy General Designer E.A. Ivanov. He was supported by the Air Force Command and the Commission of the Presidium of the Council of Ministers of the USSR (CM) on Military-Industrial Issues (MIC).[1] Following the decision of the MIC, the Air Force's Joint Committee, the testing of the T8-1 and T8-2 prototypes was headed by Air Forces Deputy Commander-in-Chief, Air Marshal N.A. Yefimov; a participant of the Great Patriotic War, a renowned ground attack pilot and twice Hero of the Soviet Union. The first pilots of the GNIKI that completed theoretical training and flew the Su-25 were: N.I. Mikhailov (25 April 1975, T8-1, flight 23), N.I. Stogov (26 July 1975, T8-1, flight 57), and A.D. Ivanov (15 August 1975, T8-1, flight 69). Other pilots from Akhtubinsk were then allowed to fly the new attack aircraft, the most prominent among them being A.A. Ivanov, V.N. Muzyka, V.A. Oleynikov, V.A. Selivanov, V.A. Solovyov and O.G. Tsoy.

By spring 1980, four T-8s had been put into the air. Two of these were T8-1D and T8-2D of the experimental production at the Moscow-based Kulon Design Bureau. The other two, T8-3 and T8-4, were produced by the Tbilisi aviation plant named after G.K. Dimitrov. The Tbilisi plant was developing serial production of the new aircraft, and several additional machines were in the final stages of construction there.[2] They were all equipped with control and recording equipment (CRA) and were also later involved in tests. The prototypes and aircraft of the developmental series were involved in aircraft development and combined during testing; the first stage of which (stage 'A') took place between 9 May 1978 and 30 May 1980.

The study of aerotechnical characteristics, weapons testing (including installation on the new Tumanskiy R-95Sh engines) and aviation systems, identified various modes of operation including the possibility of basing on unpaved airfields, et cetera. In other words, the team performed quite a comprehensive set of tests, the results of which were necessary modifications and further work carried out to improve the machine.

Operation Romb: Initial Afghan Service

Between December 1979 and February 1980, upon repeated requests from the Afghan government, the Soviet Union deployed troops to the territory of the Democratic Republic of Afghanistan (DRA). These were garrisoned around major population centres. The first year of the deployment, officially termed by the Kremlin as the 'Limited Contingent of Soviet Forces in Afghanistan' (*Ogranichenyy Kontingent Sovietskih Voysk v Afghanistanu*, OKSVA), saw an increasing scale of combat operations in the mountainous theatre. Frontline aviation was used to attack positions and infrastructure of anti-government armed units.

To provide direct support to ground troops necessitated testing (in real combat conditions), a new special-purpose Su-25 designed by the Sukhoi Design Bureau on a proactive basis. Without waiting for the 'A' stage of the testing to be completed, it was decided by order of Minister of Defence Marshal D.F. Ustinov, that the new attack aircraft should be 'battle-tested' under actual conditions of combat operations. The directive of the General Staff of the Soviet Armed Forces (GenStab) of 29 March 1980, ordered the formation of a combined Air Force and technical group.[3] This consisted of a research group and a separate experimental air squadron, which included the T-8 and Yakovlev Yak-38M vertical take-off and landing aircraft.

A view out of the left side of Su-25's cockpit, top side of a drop tank (shown foreground, low); a launch rail for the S-24 unguided rocket above it and the wing-tip housing for speed brakes – against the backdrop of the Hindu Kush Mountains.

The planes were relocated to the Shindand Air Base in the DRA. At the suggestion of the head of the Air Force Weapons Service Directorate, General A.G. Gudkov, the entire set of preparatory activities and the special tests of aircraft themselves, were given the conventional name 'Rombus' or 'Romb' (lozenge). From the GNIKI, pilots V.N. Muzyka and V.V. Solovyov flew the Su-25 prototypes; from Sukhoi Design Bureau, Ivanov and Sadovnikov. Operation Rombus has attracted much attention in the pages of aviation history books and in the memoirs of veterans, so this account will note only a few key points.

On 21 April 1980, the first two flights on aircraft T8-1D number 81 (pilot A.A. Ivanov) and T8-3 number 83 (pilot V.N. Musica) were made from the Shindand Air Base (AB). On 29 April pilots A.A. Ivanov and V.N. Musica made the first operational bombing strike, responding to a call from ground troops in the area of Chagcharan. Based on the results of the bombing strike, the headquarters of the 5th Motorised Infantry Division thanked the group.[4] During the evening formation, the group's commander, Air Major General V.V. Alfyorov, awarded the pilots Certificates of Merit 'For the First Combat Flight on a T-8 Aircraft in the DRA'.

Operation Rombus ended on 5 June 1980 and within days, the entire group had returned safely to the USSR. In a month and a half, the Rombus group had flown 100 sorties, 44 of them combat missions, from Shindand AB using prototype T8 aircraft, for a total of 98 hours and 11 minutes of flight time. Despite a number of shortcomings – in particular it was noted the ineffectiveness of airbrakes and slow throttle responsiveness of the powerplant at the high altitude and hot climate – in general, combat experience was assessed positively. Attack aircraft showed a high level of combat effectiveness, earning the most flattering assessment of the military. Correspondingly, the stage B of state joint tests officially ended with success on 30 December 1980.

Rebuilding the Attack Aviation with the Su-25

Following the results of special tests of the aeroplane, the Act of the State Commission, signed in March 1981, stated that the aeroplane's performance complied with the specified tactical and technical requirements. It recommended that the single-seat, armoured ground attack aircraft Su-25 for direct support of ground troops on the battlefield, be put into full-scale series production. The Air Forces leadership could, in the very near future, start forming the first attack aircraft units armed with the new aircraft in the Air Forces of military districts. The aircraft was nicknamed 'Rooks' by Army troops and showed excellent flight characteristics and tactical combat qualities.[5] The Dimitrov Aviation Plant in Tbilisi began serial production of the new aircraft and the rate of production gradually increased. The USSR Ministry of Defence ordered that in the very near future, the Air Forces should begin establishing the first combat units armed with Su-25 attack aircraft to be used on a large scale in Afghanistan. As a result, attack aviation, abolished in the USSR Air Forces in the early 1950s, was being revived and with a higher standard of quality.

In December 1980, Air Force Commander Air Marshal P.S. Kutahov signed a decree on the formation of the 80th Independent Attack Aviation Regiment in the Air Force of the Red Banner Transcaucasian Military District. This part-time unit was to be in the Azerbaijani SSR (Soviet Socialist Republic) at the Sital-Chai AB.[6] With one air squadron of 18 pilots, the regiment management consisted of eight pilots.

Back in the summer and autumn of 1980, on the order of the Air Force Commander of the ZakVO District, Lieutenant General G.I. Federyakov, a set of engineering staff were recruited from parts of the district along with graduates of military aviation technical schools, for the formation of engineering and aviation regiment service. There was a shortage of specialists with higher education and in the early stages, graduates of secondary aviation technical schools began to fill the positions of engineers and heads of the maintenance section. The task of studying the airframe and systems of the attack aircraft went to the aircraft factory in Tbilisi and that of studying the R-95SH engine went to the Ufa Motor Production Association. Such missions to the factories lasted 20–30 days. Among the first officers retrained on the Su-25 were:

1. Lieutenant Colonel Mirzoev Fazil Rizaevich – Deputy Regiment Commander for the aviation regiment (IAS)
2. Major Ivan Alexeyevich Kolosov – Deputy Squadron Commander for the IAS
3. Captain Shcherban Ivan Nikolaevich – Head of the Regiment's Fuel and Energy Equipment
4. Senior Lieutenant Mamontov – Chief of the Regiment's Technical Department
5. Senior Lieutenant Valery Krasnoshlykov – Head of the Maintenance Department (TEC)
6. Senior Lieutenant Victor Plakhonin – Deputy Head of the Maintenance Department
7. Senior Lieutenant Vasily Belov – aircraft technician
8. Senior Lieutenant Valery Vasilyev – aircraft technician
9. Senior Lieutenant Vitaly Viytyk – aircraft technician

In terms of geographical location (climatic conditions, territorial proximity to the manufacturing plant), the regiment's location was well-chosen. Sital-Chai airfield had a typical scheme for training airfields: the main runway had a concrete surface 2,500m long, parallel to the reserve, unpaved runway and one main taxiway, where aircraft had their starting positions or were parking. However, the material and technical base of the airfield left much to be desired, if not assessed as being in disrepair. At the beginning of January 1981, the airfield had been empty for a year, with only an air commandant's office, a separate communications and radio support battalion and a separate airfield support battalion remaining at the base.

On 4 February 1981, on the directive of the Air Force General Committee, the formation of the 80 Squadron of ZakVO Air Forces began at Sital-Chai AB. Lieutenant Colonel Anatoly Bakushev, who had previously commanded the 18th Air Force unit of the Northern Group of Forces (stationed at Shprotava, Poland), armed with Su-17 planes, was appointed as the regiment's first commander.

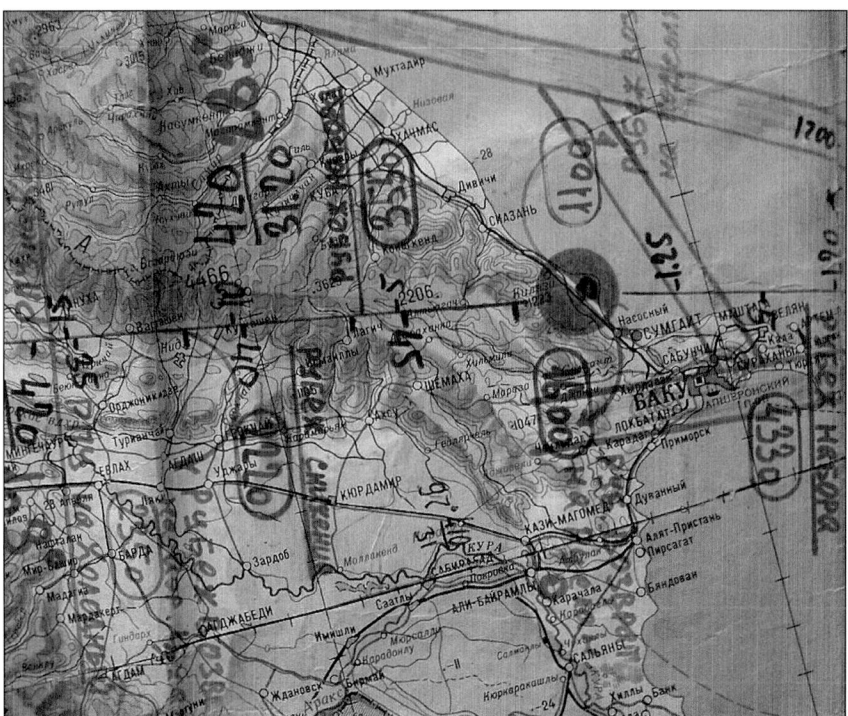
Fragment of the flight map with the area of the Sital-Chai AB.

Sital-Chai AB, satellite view.

In the early days, the main activities were the organisational and economic arrangements for accommodation, equipment for the training base and offices. For example, the Regiment headquarters (HQ) building (or what remained of it) was a pitiful sight: only walls, a roof, a few doors and windows. Therefore, the unit began accelerated repair of facilities and restoration of offices for the regiment's service chiefs. The overall amount of preparatory work was quite extensive since, in addition to the above tasks, they also had to master the Su-25 aircraft, its piloting technique and combat use. The flying staff at the regiment's formation came from various districts and units of the frontline aviation. All of the pilots had first or second Class (I and II)[7] qualifications and most were transferred, by replacement, from regiments based in European districts and from groups of troops traditionally known for their high combat readiness and training.

On 24 February 1981, the regiment's first group of air staff went to the Lipetsk Centre for theoretical retraining on combat use. The retrained air staff included the following composition:

1   Lieutenant Colonel Viktor Nikolaevich Storozhuk – Senior Inspector-Pilot of Combat Training Department of ZakVO Air Force
2   Lieutenant Colonel Bakushev Anatoly Vladimirovich – Regimental Commander
3   Lieutenant Colonel Aleksandr Mikhailovich Afanasyev – Deputy Regiment Commander for Flight Training
4   Lieutenant Colonel Alexander Antonovich Khovrin – senior navigator of the regiment
5   Major Bardintsev Yuri Timofeyevich – Regiment Chief of Political Department
6   Major Grigoriev Yuri Anatolievich – Head of the Regimental Gunfire and Tactical Training
7   Captain Korovin Nikolay Viktorovich – regimental intelligence chief
8   Major Khanarin Vladimir Nikolaevich – Squadron Commander
9   Captain Anatoly Korobkin – Deputy Squadron Commander
10 Major Boris Kozyrev – Deputy Squadron Commander for Political Affairs
11 Major Loshakov Alexander Alekseevich – Squadron Chief of Staff
12 Captain Tikhonov Yuri Anatolievich – Squadron Commander
13 Captain Nikolai Ivanovich Shulimov – Commander of a *zveno* (four-ship tactical formation)
14 Captain Valery Alexandrovich Arevkov – Commander of a *zveno*
15 Captain Dyakov Mikhail Evgenyevich – senior pilot
16 Captain Tsygankov Nikolay Vasilievich – senior pilot
17 Senior Lieutenant Sergey Vasilyevich Prichinenko – pilot
18 Senior Lieutenant Rafael Rifovich Yakupov – pilot

Pilots who were 'pioneers' in attack jet aviation mostly flew the Sukhoi Su-17M3s, Su-17M2s and Su-17Ms, with the exception of Major Grigoryev and Captain Arevkov, who had previously flown the Mikoyan i Gurevich MiG-21, and Captain Shulimov, who flew the Mikoyan i Gurevch MiG-17. The materiel in Lipetsk was studied only from schemes and photographs. The specifics of piloting technique and flight operation were studied according to methodological recommendations developed by specialists of the Sukhoi Aircraft Design Bureau and the State Research Institute of the Air Force. By April 1981, in order to organise the flights at the airfield, the Commander of Air Forces of Transcaucasian Military District submitted 'Instruction on flights at Sital-Chai airfield' and, by May 1981, 'Instruction on the combat use of aircraft at the Nasosniy AB, 35km northwest of Baku'. However, the main difficulty was the lack of most of the necessary methodological literature and guidance documents. After theoretical retraining, the practical mastery of the attack aircraft had to be started as soon as possible. However, there were no Su-25 aircraft at Sital-Chai.

Anatoly Bakushev
Born 18 April 1946, after leaving school in 1963, he entered Yeysk Higher Military Aviation School of Pilots. Upon the completion of training in 1967, he was sent to serve in the Far East in 523rd *aviatsionnyy polk istrebiteley-bombardirovshchikov* (FBA Regiment, APIB).[8] After five years of service, he entered the Air Force Academy and continued to fly in the Pre-Carpathian region of Lutsk and later in Poland. In 1981, he was appointed commander of the 80th Squadron of the Su-25 in Sital-Chai. From 1984 until 1985 he participated in the combat operations in the DRA as commander of 378th Independent Reconnaissance Squadron. After Afghanistan, Bakushev served in the Baltic States and commanded a division in Mongolia. In 1992, he graduated from the General Staff Academy and continued to serve in the General Staff of the Air Force. He retired from the Air Force with the rank of Major General from the post of Head of Combat Training of Frontline Aviation. He died on 12 October 2014.

The first commander of the 80th Brigade Combat Team, A.V. Bakushev.

Nikolay Korovin recalled:

After theoretical retraining in March, a business trip was organised to the Georgiy Dimitrov Aircraft Factory in Tbilisi, which produced the Su-25 aircraft. After a tour of the plant's workshops, we saw the aircraft for the first time 'live' and sat in the cockpit. The test pilot, Selivanov, conducted a demonstration flight for us. We watched the take-off, turns in flight and manoeuvre configuration of the wing mechanics, piloting and landing. Of course, we were impressed. After doing the ground training and passing the credits, on arrival at the duty station we started the flights. The first flights of the 80th Regiment took place on 7 April 1981. The Regiment had not yet received Su-25 aeroplanes, so the flying staff performed flights on previously mastered types. For that purpose, two Su-17UM3 twins, two Su-17M3s and two Su-17M2s were transferred from Bolshiye Shiraki airfield to Sital-Chai airfield'.

In the meantime, the first batch of attack aircraft was flown in Tbilisi and taken up by the military acceptance department of the plant. However, it turned out that it was impossible to prepare the aircraft for delivery to the customer either at the plant, where the targeting equipment testing areas were not yet ready, or at the regiment, where the MEC had not yet been properly formed. The Air Forces Commander-in-Chief, P.S. Kutakhov, proposed to the Chief Designer E.A. Ivanov to take the planes to the Akhtubinsk branch of the Sukhoi Flight Research Institute where specialists from the Design Bureau and the Institute were able to carry out the work.

Nikolay Korovin

Captain N.V. Korovin.

Upon graduation from Yeyanskoye Higher Military Aviation School in 1976, Nikolay Korovin was assigned to 67th Branch of 76 Military Aviation of the Leningrad Oblast Military District. He completed the steps from pilot to commander of a flight. In February 1981, at the rank of Captain, he was appointed head of reconnaissance of 80 Squadron of Air Forces of ZakVO. He participated in combat operations in the DRA from May 1981 until September 1982 as deputy commander of 200 Squadron. Since November 1982, he continued to serve in the 80th Squadron as deputy commander of the air squadron, chief of flights. From August 1984, as a Major, he was Commander of the 166th Squadron of the Aviation Squadron of the Air Force of the ZakVO Air Forces, and then as a Lieutenant Colonel from February 1987. From November 1988, Nikolay Korovin served as senior navigator of the regiment and from November 1989, senior navigator of the Air Force division (97th Airborne Division). In October 1993, he was dismissed from the Armed Forces with the rank of Lieutenant Colonel.[9]

The first flights of the 80th Squadron at the Sital-Chai AB, 7 April 1981.

Speech by Colonel A.V. Bakushev, commander of the 80th Brigade Combat Team, on the day of the departure of the 200th Brigade Combat Team to the DRA, 18 June 1981.

After the targeting sights had been adjusted, the aeroplanes were flown at the local training area by the test pilots of the Design Bureau and the GNIKI, before being handed over to the 80th Squadron. To aid in the practical development of the Su-25, Sukhoi Design Bureau set up and seconded to Sital-Chai on 10 April 1981, an aviation maintenance crew headed by leading designer N.T. Zhelamsky, plus warranty and technical crews from the Tbilisi aviation plant to provide maintenance for the aircraft for the first flights. The new aircraft had a two-year warranty (up to 225 flight hours) and all failures had to be rectified on site by factory representatives.

On 14 April 1981, the first Su-25s of the 01 series were brought to the Sital-Chai airfield, and on 20 April, the regiment started to fly them for the first time. N.V. Korovin recalled:

The Su-25s were flown on 20 April, with Lieutenant Colonel V.N. Storozhuk, Major V.N. Khanarin and Captain N.V. Korovin taking the first flight shift on the Su-25. The consultants were the test pilots of the 8th GNIKI Air Forces, Colonel I.O. Tsoy and Lieutenant Colonel V.V. Solovyov, who took part in Operation Rombus in 1980. Colonels Danilevsky and Timkov, pilots of the Lipetsk Centre for training and retraining of flight personnel, flew together with the regiment's pilots on the Su-25. They were preparing material for the writing of the *Methodological manual on piloting techniques for the Su-25 aircraft*. True, they were a little behind us. By the time they were practising the recommendations on taking off in pairs, we were already flying in groups to the range. So, when mastering the Su-25, we only had one book –*The Su-25 Pilot's Manual*. True, there was also the *Programme for flying the Su-25 following maintenance work and engine changes*, but that was only used by those pilots who flew the planes. The new aircraft was initially perceived ambiguously. Unfamiliar was the presence of two twin-rotor engines, the leaky cabin, the lack of an air system on the aircraft, and especially the hydraulic foot brakes, which took some getting used to, plus the good visibility from the cockpit. There were also peculiarities of the aircraft's characteristics. Short take-off and landing distances improved lateral stability (the first series of aircraft did not have boosters in the aileron control channel), and good rate of climb. Its protection was also impressive. The aircraft had an armoured cockpit, an armoured visor protecting the pilot's head and a rescue parachute, armoured plates protecting the engines from below, large diameter steering control rods, redundant cable guidance, and fuel tanks filled with polyurethane foam.

Technical crews of the 80th OShAE commenced flight support training with factory specialists. Upon completion, a test was held according to the results of which aircraft technicians (No. 01 V. Viityk, No. 02 V. Vasilyev, and No. 03 V. Belov) were allowed to independently service the T-8 product.

Preparation for Return to Afghanistan

On 28 April 1981, the regiment was visited by the Deputy Commander of the Air Force, twice Hero of the Soviet Union, Air Marshal A.N. Yefimov. The renowned attack pilot from the Great Patriotic War personally supervised the programme. Active combat operations were conducted in Afghanistan where the troops were in urgent need of an attack aircraft. The regiment, at full strength, was planned to be transferred to the territory of DRA. However, it was short of both equipment and trained personnel.

The number of aircraft produced by the Tbilisi aviation plant was in single figures and there were barely enough retrained pilots for a squadron. Nevertheless, the Ministry of Defence and Minister D.F. Ustinov decided to set a task, which A.N. Yefimov presented to the Air Force Command of the ZakVO District and the 80th Regiment leadership: as soon as possible to prepare the flying staff for combat operations in pairs, collect the engineering staff, receive and prepare the material for the deployment of an attack aviation regiment in the 40th Army Air Force.

When it became clear that the number of aircraft to staff the regiment was not enough, the plan for an independent attack squadron and support units were developed, combined with an independent company of ground support and an independent communications platoon for radio support. The unit was given its official designation: 200th Independent Attack Aviation Squadron (OShAE).

At the base of the regiment and the training grounds of the district, work intensified. Thorough training was conducted day and night for combat operations in the DRA which involved the test pilots of 8th GNIKI from Akhtubinsk, flight instructors of the 4th Centre for Combat Employment and Retraining of Personnel (4th TsBP i PLS) from Lipetsk, as well as specialists of Sukhoi and the manufacturer. To assist in the formation of the squadron, a group of generals and officers of the Air Forces General Staff, headed by Deputy Commander-in-Chief of the Air Forces, Air Marshal Yefimov, worked in the regiment. On 8 May 1981, the second group of the regiment's flying personnel was flown to Lipetsk for retraining:

1. Captain Grigori Nikolaevich Garus – Squadron Commander
2. Captain Yuri Anatolievich Roslyakov – pilot
3. Captain Sidorov Vladimir Nikolaevich – senior pilot
4. Senior Lieutenant Vladimir Vladimirovich Bondarenko – pilot
5. Senior Lieutenant Yuri Romanov – Senior Airman
6. Senior Lieutenant Anatoly Lavrenko – pilot
7. Senior Lieutenant Vladimir Aleksandrovich Shchelkov – pilot
8. Senior Lieutenant Eugene Jasinski – pilot

The group underwent accelerated retraining and as early as 16 May, the pilots started flying from the Sital-Chai airfield.

By the summer of that year the plant was able to prepare and deliver only 11 attack aircraft of production series 01 to the Air Force: one aircraft manufactured in Q4 (fourth quarter) 1980 and 10 aircraft manufactured in Q1 and Q2 of 1981. In the absence of a sufficient number of serial machines, with the aim of manning the air squadron to its full strength of 12 combat units, the formation group included a prototype of the serial production T8-6 aircraft (construction number 25508101006) having temporarily removed it from the 'B' phase programme.

Instead of the assigned Bort 86, the aircraft was marked with 12. The first three T-8s arrived at Sital-Chai on 14 April and were taken over by the plant's pilots V.E. Bazalyuk, I.P. Bessonov and E.V. Komov. The flights commenced on 20 April and the flying staff of the regiment began their practical training with the attack aircraft. The remaining nine aircraft were delivered to the 80th Squadron by mid-May.

The Su-25 attack aircraft had standard factory camouflage paintwork: the sides of the fuselage and vertical tail, the upper surfaces of the fuselage, wing and horizontal tail were painted in protective enamel with margins and patches of light green, sandy and brown. The lower surfaces of the fuselage, wing and horizontal tail were blue-grey. The state identification marking, the 'five-pointed star' red with a white-red border, was located in six positions: on the wing surfaces at the bottom and top and on the vertical fins on both sides. Tactical numbers 01 to 12 were applied in red with a white outline on the sides of the cockpit, under the hinged part of the canopy.

The squadron's training intensity increased sharply when the aircraft were increased to full strength of 12 combat units, with three to four training flights per day. From the outset, the training of pilots on the Su-25 aeroplane was aimed at preparing them for combat operations in Afghanistan. This training took place in the mountainous conditions of the eastern spurs of the Caucasus Range, both at the firing and tactical ranges.

In early June, Air Marshal A.N. Yefimov paid another visit to the regiment. At a five-minute meeting attended by the district aviation command and the 80th Squadron headquarters, the issue was raised of the appointment of the commander of the attack squadron to be sent to Afghanistan. The candidacy of Lieutenant Colonel A.M. Afanasyev, Deputy Regimental Commander in charge of flight training, was supported almost unanimously.

Major B.V. Kozyrev was appointed deputy political officer of the squadron, Major Belousov as Chief of Staff and Major I.A. Kolosov was deputy squadron commander for aviation engineering service (IAS). Once this portion of the unit was completed, the regiment personnel were assembled to set the task and select and approve candidates to be sent to the DRA.

By mid-June, the formation of the 200th Separate Attack Aircraft Squadron and its preparation for combat operations in the DRA with Su-25 attack aircraft, was virtually completed. The training was completed by two tactical flight exercises (LTE) of the squadron on 9 and 11 June. On 16 and 17 June, the squadron made flying missions with external fuel tanks to check their depletion, after which it was fully ready for redeployment. A total of 625 flights had been made for a total of 365 hours flight time. The next day, the flight to the territory of the DRA was planned. The place for deployment of the unit was determined to be Shindand airfield, town and centre of Shindand district, Herat province, in the west of the country.

Deployment

In the period from 18 to 19 June, 200 Squadron, commanded by Lieutenant Colonel A.M. Afanasyev, was redeployed to the DRA

Alexander Mikhailovich Afanasyev

Born on 9 January 1946, in 1968 Afanasyev graduated from the Kharkov Higher Military Aviation School, named after twice Hero of the Soviet Union S.I. Gritsvetsev. He was then assigned to the fighter aviation regiment of the Transcaucasian Military District of the Red Banner. Since 1978, his service included the 189th Guards Attack Aviation Regiment of the Transbaikal Military District in the Borzya settlement. Afanasyev passed all stages, from pilot to squadron commander. In 1981, he was appointed deputy commander of the Sital-Chai regiment (80th Squadron of the Air Force of the Red Banner of the ZakVO). From 1981 until 1982, he participated in combat operations in the DRA as commander of 200th Independent Attack Aviation Squadron. After completing this mission, he served as senior inspector-pilot of the Air Safety Service of the Air Force until April 1986. In 1992, he retired from the Armed Forces with the rank of Colonel.

The combat composition of 200th OShAE at the time of departure for the DRA was:

1. Lieutenant Colonel Alexander Mikhailovich Afanasyev – Air Force Commander
2. Major Boris Vasilyevich Kozyrev – deputy commander
3. Captain Korovin Nikolai Vasilievich – deputy commander
4. Captain Anatoly Korobkin – navigator
5. Captain Mikhail Yevgenyevich Dyakov – senior pilot, Chief of Parachute Department
6. Senior Airman Major Loshakov Aleksandr Alekseevich – Weapons Systems Officer
7. 1st Flight
   a. Captain Grigory Garus – commander of the platoon
   b. Captain Roslyakov Yuri Anatolievich – pilot
   c. Captain Sidorov Vladimir – senior pilot, head of reconnaissance
   d. Senior Lieutenant Bondarenko Vladimir Vladimirovich – pilot
8. 2nd Flight
   a. Captain Tikhonov Yuri Anatolievich – commander of the platoon
   b. Senior Lieutenant Sergey Prichinenko – pilot
   c. Captain Nikolay Tsygankov – senior pilot
   d. Senior Lieutenant Vladimir Shchelkov– pilot
9. 3rd Flight
   a. Captain Nikolai Ivanovich Shulimov– platoon commander
   b. Senior Lieutenant Evgeny Yasinsky – pilot
   c. Senior Lieutenant Yury Romanov – senior pilot
   d. Senior Lieutenant Anatoly Lavrenko – pilot

---

at Shindand airfield and began to fight in the 40th Army Air Force. After the squadron departed for Afghanistan, only a part-time regimental headquarters, several pilots and factory specialists remained in Sital-Chai. The management faced the same tasks: staffing the regiment with personnel and equipment, retraining for a new type of aviation equipment and maintenance of flight skills.

In September 1981, the 80th Squadron began to receive aviation personnel from other aviation regiments in preparation for the replacement of 200th OShAE personnel in Afghanistan the following year. As the withdrawal of the unit's Su-25s meant the regiment was left without aircraft of this type, six Su-17M3s were temporarily seconded from Shirak and ETS were urgently (in a few days) retrained on them and began to fly.

In April 1982, the Komsomolsk-on-Amur plant received four Su-17UM3 aircraft, with the new Su-25 arriving from Tbilisi Aircraft Plant in May 1982. They began arriving in the form of transfer flights, undertaken from Monday to Saturday, with Sunday (rarely a Saturday) being designated as a day off. In September 1982, the second shift of 200th Squadron (Squadron Commander Major V. Khanarin) left for Shindand.

From October 1982 the 80th Squadron became a two-squadron regiment and began to prepare for the new replacement of 200 Squadron (Squadron Commander, Major P.V. Ruban). From then onwards, the 80th Attack Aviation Regiment (one squadron, rotational shifts) continued combat operations in the DRA until the formation in November 1984 of the 80th Squadron (regimental command, fuel and maintenance organisation, and one squadron) and 200th Squadron of the 90th Squadron (airfield Artsiz, Odessa military district) of 378th Independent Attack Aviation Regiment of the 40th Army Air Force.

Shrouded Su-25 at the parking lot of the Sital-Chai AB.

CHAPTER 2
IN SPECIAL CIRCUMSTANCES

On 18 June 1981, the redeployment began of personnel, aircraft and ground support equipment of the 200th OShAE to the DRA. Su-25 attack aircraft and Su-17UM3 combat trainers flew in formations from Sital-Chai to Kizil-Arvat escorted by An-12s with forward deployed teams and aircraft receiving and releasing groups. The initial plan was to relocate in one day, but unforeseen technical difficulties forced the group to spend the night at a transit airfield.

Next day, 19 June, the planes flew to Shindand airbase with an intermediate stop at Mary airfield. The next flight was followed by the An-26 which was flown by Air Marshal A.N. Yefimov, who accompanied the squadron throughout the flight. One year after the end of the 'Romb' operation, the new operation, codenamed Romb-2, was launched – unofficial military testing of the Su-25 in combat conditions, the basic name being 'Examination'. This historic date was, in fact, the beginning of the assault aircraft's operational history.

Organisationally, the 200th Squadron reported directly to the 40th Army Air Forces Headquarters. The squadron had 12 Su-25s, two Su-17UM3s and 18 pilots assigned to the squadron's directorate and three flights. The unit's aviation engineering service included engineers in the following specialists: aircraft and engine, armament, avionics, electronics; maintenance teams in the roles of team leaders, technicians and aircraft mechanics; unit technicians, aircraft technicians and aircraft mechanics. The technical and operational unit consisted of maintenance and repair groups, where the Maintenance Department included the mechanics and test stand-groups, responsible for engines.

Settling In

The artificial (concrete) runway of the Shindand airfield was located at an elevation of 1,158m above sea level and measured 2,700 × 48m. The squadron was stationed in the Soviet zone near the runway's northern end. Units of the Democratic Republic of Afghanistan Air Force (DRAAF) were based near the southern end of the strip. The joint deployment of Soviet and Afghan aircraft at most airfields, enabled closer cooperation between them. This shortened the reaction time thus increasing their combat effectiveness. Aircraft were dispersed within blast pents which, essentially, consisted of a tie-down apron paved with perforated metal plates, surrounded from three sides by an earthen berm. There was also a headquarters, a tent camp with

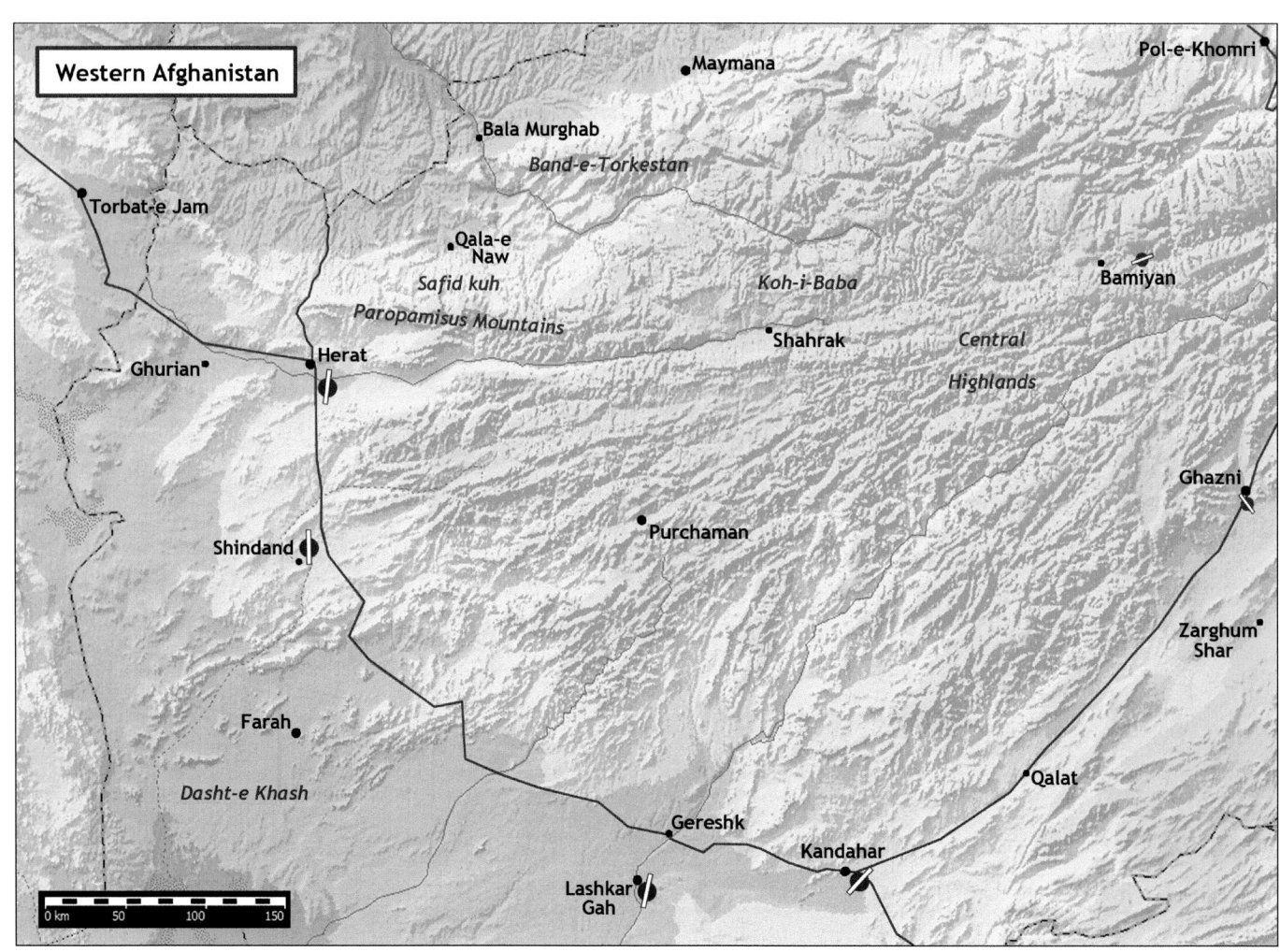

A map of western Afghanistan with the Shindand AB. (Map by Tom Cooper)

a canteen for conscripts, a fuel and energy supply unit (based on vehicles) and a bathhouse. The officers lived in a panelled module opposite the shop, in rooms of several people to each one.

There was not much time to get it all up and running. On 25 June the first flights were made to familiarise pilots with the air base and the area of operations. In early July, they began flights for combat use. The territory of operations within responsibility of the Aviation Group West – the main base of which was the Shindand AB – included western and southwestern provinces of Afghanistan: Badghis, Herat, Farah and Helmand. In latitude, this extended from the Soviet border between Turagundi and Kushka, to the south of Afghanistan (the desert regions of Zaranja, Girishka and Lashkar Gah) and in longitude, from the Iranian border to the mountainous Chaghcharan.

The troop contingent in the area had been considerably reinforced during the past year since the end of Operation Romb. Apart from the 5th Guards' Zimovnikovsky Red Banner, Order of Kutuzov, II Class Motorised Rifle Division (commanded by Colonel B.V. Gromov), involved in combat operations were the 103rd Guards Red Banner, Order of Lenin, Order of Kutuzov, II Class Airborne Division (commanded by Major General I.F. Ryabchenko, replaced in September by Major General A.E. Sliusar) and 21 Infantry Brigade of the armed forces of the DRA.

The 200th OShAE was quite calm in this period as there were no aerial incursions from Iran yet, nor movement of the Mujahideen caravans from that direction. The main traffic came from Pakistan, the districts of Kandahar in the southeast and Kapisa and Parwan in the northeast, via the famous Panjshir Ravine.[1] To enable it to operate in regions far removed from Shindand, the Su-25 was now equipped with two PTB-800 drop tanks with capacity of 800-litre. As a result, the range of the aircraft with a combat load was as much as 400km, enabling the attack aircraft to be engaged first in strikes in the region of Kandahar, the second largest and most important city in the country and then to operate from Bagram and Kabul airfields with short-time redeployments.

Into Action

At the beginning of September, a large scale military operation was conducted in the area of Farah, in the mountain massif of Lurkoh, by units of the 5th Motorised Rifle Division. The powerful fortification was one of the base camps of the Mujahideen,[2] whose units offered stubborn resistance to the Soviet troops. In the course of combat operations that lasted several days and were accompanied by artillery and air support including Su-25 aircraft, the enemy suffered serious casualties and was forced to withdraw from the region. During the operation, the deputy commander of the VVS in the Soviet Republic of Turkmenistan, Major General V.N. Khakhalov, was killed. He had arrived in Shindand on instructions from the Air Force Commander-in-Chief to assess the effectiveness of the attack aircraft operating in the area on behalf of the 5th Motorised Infantry Division.

The fourth offensive into Panjshir, codenamed 'Canyon', began on 6 September 1981. Aircraft support was provided mainly in the area where the 70th Motorised Rifle Brigade was deployed in mountainous terrain which had a high concentration of Dushman strongholds. They performed the task of covering the infantry

> From the book *Limited Contingent* by B.V. Gromov:
> General Khakhalov flew to Afghanistan having received an order from Air Force Commander Marshal P.S. Kutakhov to check the effectiveness of Su-25 attack aircraft in this mountainous area. At first, there was a serious fight over not carrying out this order, because according to Kutakhov's plan, after each bombing and attack from the air, the motorised rifle units had to go to the centre of Lurkokh to make sure that the Air Force had achieved its objective. The command of the 5th Division, and the 40th Army as a whole, was by no means happy with this – we knew what such a 'check' would lead to, and we already had bitter experience of losses.
>
> For several days General Khakhalov was near Lurkoha. We prevented him in every possible way from flying into the centre of the mountain range. Nevertheless, he chose the moment when I left and my deputy continued to lead the combat operations and, despite persistent advice not to do so, at his own risk he flew in two helicopters deep into the mountain gorges of Lurkokh on September 5, 1981. From there Khakhalov never returned. In this combat mission, the general attacked an identified mobile target, and on leaving the attack, the helicopter in which he was riding was shot down by the dushmans and crashed not far from their base. After this happened, we were simply forced with fierce fighting to fight our way through the mountains and ridges, along the bottom of two gorges into the centre of the mountain range. A very quickly prepared operation was carried out mainly, of course, to retrieve at least the bodies of the General and the crew members who had died with him, and not to leave them to be desecrated. When we reached the centre of Lurkoha and finally captured this stronghold, the wreckage of a downed helicopter and the remains of the officers were found not far from the base. They were terrifying to look at. The bodies of the general, who was in uniform, and the helicopter pilots had been brutally mocked by the dushmans – their eyes had been poked out and their ears cut off…[3]

from the air and supporting the offensive of Soviet troops. Working in narrow gorges from strongholds located in old fortresses since the times of war with English colonists, demanded great courage, flying skills and maximum concentration of attention from pilots.

The attack aircraft were highly praised by the forward air gunners. Acting directly in combat units, they requested support from the air, gave targeting instructions and figuratively speaking, served as the 'eyes' of the pilots in orientation, constructing the attack and assessing its results. After the helicopters, which demonstrated the best coherence and interaction with troops, the Su-25 was the most sought-after aerial fire support vehicle, prized above all for its armament power and accuracy. There is a practice of assigning call signs to aircraft required for radio communication with ground troops. As long ago as 1980, the Su-25 attack aircraft was given the nickname 'Haircomb' (*Raschoska*), for its distinctive appearance from the ground, by spotters. Airfield witticisms dubbed the unusual contours of the plane 'the humpbacked one'.

The main methods of combat operations by Su-25s in Afghanistan were:

Flight personnel of the 200the OShAE with Marshal Yefimov and officers of the 80th Attack Aviation Regiment and ZakVO Air Forces on the eve of their departure for the DRA. Sital-Chai, 1981.From left to right in the first row of the photo: second A. Bakushev, A. Afanasyev, fourth E. Shubin (Deputy Commander of the ZakVO Air Forces on combat training), centre Marshal A. Yefimov, eigth Yu. Bardintsev, and nineth V. Storozhuk (combat training department of ZakVO Air Forces). Second row: B.V. Kozyrev, Y.A. Tikhonov, A.S. Lavrenko, N.V. Korovin, S.V. Prichinenko, A.I. Korobkin, V. Shelkov, and on the far right G.N. Garus. Third row: V. Sidorov, N.I. Shulimov, E. Yasinsky, Y. Roslyakov, V.V. Bondarenko, Y. Romanov, N.V. Tsygankov, and M.E. Dyakov.

Aerial view of the Shindand Aerodrome as of the early 1980s.

Personnel of the 200th OShAE and civilian personnel in Shindand.

- Strikes against pre-selected ground targets to provide air support to ground forces in counter-insurgency operations and actions against newly identified targets
- Direct support – covering convoys on marches and escorting troops on raids
- Reconnaissance and strike action – the so-called 'free hunt'
- Laying mines on caravan trails, supply routes, bases and rebel locations

Attack Methodology

Combat tasks for air strikes on assigned targets came from the 40th Army Air Forces Headquarters by combat orders down the chain of command, via datalinks. They contained the coordinates of the targets, a brief description, the force required and information stating there were no civilians within 500m of the target. In accordance with the orders, tasking maps were prepared then the combat load and parametres for the use of weapons were determined. The Su-25 attack aircraft flew both as part of mixed air groups – mostly in combination with their 'colleagues' – their neighbours at the airfield, the Su-17 fighter-bombers of the 217th APIB – and on their own.

When carrying out complex strikes as part of strike and support groups, the sequence of actions was usually as follows: Air defence suppression groups (one or two pairs of fighter-bombers) covered the area. Next, the target designation group (a pair of Mi-8s with an air gunner onboard, or a pair of fighter-bombers) marked targets with bombs or unguided rockets. Four to six Su-25 attack aircraft would be part of the main strike group. Following an interval between groups of 1–2 minutes, they would unload up to 25 tonnes of lethal metal on the enemy per flight.

Photographic control of the strike was carried out by MiG-21R reconnaissance aircraft or Mi-8 helicopters, equipped with AFA-42/100 cameras and RA-39 hand-held aerial cameras. Search and rescue support was provided by a pair of Mi-8s hovering at a safe altitude in the area of the strike. However, it should be noted that strikes in mixed groups entailed an increased risk of fire from the ground for aircraft behind the lead group, often the not-too-fast Su-25. The organisation of such strikes was also fraught with difficulties in terms of command and communications. Later on, practice showed that it was more practical (and effective) to carry out combat missions in separate groups – crews from the same squadron or regiment. When fighting against fortifications and caves in the mountains, the time required to strike was minimal as the enemy, taking advantage of the terrain, could easily disperse and take cover. As manoeuvring was limited, the groups consisted of one or two pairs of attack aircraft. The lead attacked first while the wingman, following at a distance, provided cover, attacked, and both came out of the dive with a counter-dive manoeuvre. In open terrain, it was possible to attack the target and get out from almost any direction. In the mountain gorges, the fighters zeroed in on the sectors from where the combat aircraft could escape and they waited. The density of fire in such cases was very high: vehicles often returned to base with combat damage.

V. Sidorov in the cockpit of the Su-25 Bort Number 04 preparing to take off.

The following air weapons were used against soft targets and enemy manpower: 30mm aerial gun VPU-17A, RBK cluster bomb units (CBUs), unguided rockets S-5, S-8, S-24 with non-contact radio detonators (detonation height 15–30m), S-24s with contact fuses for attacks on fortifications and well-protected targets (like firing points constructed into the solid rock or ammunition depots inside caves), general-purpose aerial bombs (FAB), and OFAB high explosive/fragmentation bombs calibre 250 or 500kg. The most-effective were the S-24 rockets, which combined a high power of impact and accuracy. Firing them from 2,000 metres away, experienced pilots would regularly place their hits within 10-15m from the target. The explosive power of the S-24 had a piercing effect on rock and concrete shelters, and 4,000 fragments dispersed giving a continuous area of damage within a radius of 30–40 metres.

Air support for convoys with soft and armoured vehicles was provided from the airfield duty position. For such missions, Su-25s usually deployed UB-32-57 or B-8 pods for unguided rockets calibres 57 and 80mm, respectively, sometimes FAB-250 bombs. When the forces on duty were called in, bombing missions were carried out at dominant heights located at a distance of 1,500–2,000m from the route of the columns, as well as firing unguided rockets along the columns at locations on both sides of the roads from where countermeasures were observed.

The 'free hunting' flights were preceded by thorough preparations. The area and location of Soviet troops and enemy forces were studied using maps and photographic records, intelligence and communications were also analysed. The search for caravans, vehicles and Mujahideen camps was conducted at altitudes of 600–1,200m at speeds of 600–700km/h. The simultaneous attack was carried out overtly in pairs so as not to allow the fighters to use natural shelters, followed by a change of combat course by 50–60 degrees and a new approach to the target. The combat load on the RUD sorties included 250 and 500kg bombs, RBKs, B-8 or UB-32-57 pods.

When moving single objects were detected, radio communication was used to ask the command post if there were any Soviet troops or 'democrats' in the area. If information was received that no Soviet or Afghan troops were present, the target was destroyed on the second approach after the contour of the strike had been built. Sometimes it was impossible to identify the exact identity of the target – the remoteness and the mountains impaired radio communication – and the decision had to be made by the crews.

This led to various consequences, for example; they reported an attack on a target which later turned out to be a bus carrying civilians. Other pilots, being afraid of punishment, were silent about the defeat of an unknown jeep – it turned out that US and Pakistani military advisers had been killed in it. The army command was looking for the 'authors' to be presented with an award, but never found its heroes.

Paying a Price

From the very first days, the attack aircraft were actively engaged by air defence equipment, primarily small arms, but also the time-honoured DShK heavy machine gun. The cockpit on the Su-25 was sufficiently well-protected – on the ground, multiple large-calibre gunfire marks would be found on the frontal and side armour plates – but, other aircraft parts, mainly the wings, remained vulnerable as they had the largest surface area. Many Su-25s would return to departure airfields with more serious damage and in some cases, pilots had to land the aircraft with only one engine running.

During Operation Canyon in September 1981, pilot Senior Lieutenant A.S. Lavrenko carried out an attack on a ZPU machine gun. The strike destroyed the target but the Su-25 also sustained combat damage to a wing fuel tank and control wiring. The aircraft caught fire at an altitude of 2,500 metres. Manoeuvring in the air, the pilot succeeded in knocking down the flames and made a successful landing at the airfield of departure.

On 25 November 1981, the ground attack aircraft construction number 25508101018, piloted by G.N. Garus, was hit by a DShK into the left engine. As result, the hydraulic system malfunctioned and the aircraft had to land without mechanisation of the wing and brake pads. The aircraft was evacuated from the runway and upon inspection on parking, found to have torn holes in the nacelle skin and bulkheads with a cross-section size of 5 to 20cm.

The very next day, 26 November, Senior Lieutenant V.V. Bondarenko found himself in a similar situation. After completing his combat mission, Bondarenko's Su-25 (construction number 25508101021) with hydraulic and electric wiring damaged, threatened to catch fire at any moment. Yet, he returned safely to his base airfield on the remaining fuel. The aircraft was soon recovered but in its first combat flight after repairs in December 1981, the same Bondarenko came under even heavier anti-aircraft fire. With failing control of the aircraft, the pilot began his approach. During landing gear deployment, due to damaged hydraulics, one flap suddenly retracted spontaneously while the other remained in the same position. The attack aircraft began to roll and only Bondarenko's skill made it possible to land. However, the hard touch-down caused further damage and the aircraft was out of action for a long time.

The danger in the air to the Su-25 was posed not only by enemy fire but also by a design feature of the aircraft. It lacked power boosters in the lateral control channel. The situation changed rapidly during combat, pilots were always able to meet the maximum speed limit of 850km/h with a g-load of five. As a result, in such conditions, the effectiveness of the servo compensators decreased causing them to stop and jam, resulting in ineffective ailerons. The aircraft lost control and went into a roll. One such situation, during a dive at a target with increasing speed, nearly resulted in the downfall of Major G.N. Garus, but fortunately, he was able to get the attack aircraft out of the dangerous position.

A huge burden rested on the shoulders of the aviation engineering service headed by Major Ivan Alekseevich Kolosov, who ensured the serviceability of the aircraft and maintained its combat readiness at the appropriate level. Working selflessly, virtually without days off, were aircraft technicians A. Ageyev, P. Akulov, P. Bychok, V. Vasiliev, V. Viytyk, Ilyin, A. Kalashnikov, K. Lapshin, A. Novikov, V. Plakhonin, and Samuleyev, all under the leadership of different department chiefs and engineers of the squadron, including V. Belov, A. Anfimichev, Krasnoshlykov, and V. Podzolkov. Thanks to their efforts, on average it took them 25 minutes to prepare a *zveno* of attack aircraft for a second flight without any mechanical equipment.

Specialists of the power plant, headed by V. Karasev, promptly repaired damage and aircraft were put back into operation in the shortest time possible despite the shortage of spare parts, consumables and equipment. Invaluable assistance to the squadron's engineering staff was provided by representatives of the Sukhoi Aviation Plant (specialists in aircraft maintenance, targeting equipment and armament) and the warranty team,[4] through which a steady supply of damaged and out of service units and assemblies from the plant was organised.

It is well known that instructions and manuals in aviation are 'written in blood' and the slightest failure to comply with them or carelessness and negligence in the operation of complex aircraft, often led to disastrous consequences. On 16 October 1981, at around 08.00 Kabul time, during scheduled flights, technician Lieutenant P.I. Akulov approached the engine inlet of the Su-25 bort number 10 to check the sighting and navigation system before the squadron's technical officer, Major A.A. Loshakov, went to fly. He was pulled into the inlet and as a result of exposure to significant suffocation and contact with rapidly rotating parts of the first stage of the engine compressor he, 'sustained multiple injuries incompatible with life'.

Aircraft Technician Lieutenant Anatoly Novikov at the entrance to 'his' protective blast pent No. 04.

Aircraft Technician Lieutenant Anatoly Novikov with his Su-25, Bort Number 04.

Vitaliy Viytyk, a technician of aircraft 200 OShAE, a Senior Lieutenant, recollected:

I went to Afghanistan as an aircraft technician for aircraft 09. The airfield of Shindand is more than 1,000 metres above sea level. Climatic conditions are harsh: heat in summer, cold in winter. Water is brought in, the food in the canteen is terrible: all year-round stew, dry potatoes, liquid oil with flies. We were surviving with the help of paraffin primus, which we used to cook fish soup from canned fish. Typhus, malaria and jaundice were widespread diseases – some were repeatedly ill. I was ill with typhoid. I was treated in the hospital for 11 days: my doctor was an ear- nose and throat specialist and we lived in a tent. For the first time I saw pills of levomycetin, with which we were treated, in huge plastic bags. Diet [was] semolina boiled in water, twice a day. Treatment was voluntary – once every few days the doctor came and poured a mountain of levomycetin on the table. As a result, my medical record said, 'acute respiratory infections'. The working day started at five in the morning and ended, as a rule, at one or two in the morning. Often aircraft technicians would spend the night inside aircraft cockpits. There were days when two sections of aircraft would drop up to 100 tons of cargo. Between sorties everyone, including pilots, was engaged in hanging ammunition … I participated in the operation from Bagram airfield, as well as in demonstration of aviation equipment in Kabul to Babrak Karmal. Our air squadron lost three men: a conscript soldier shot himself on the first day of arrival; Lieutenant P. Akulov was killed after being ingested into an engine at the maintenance post; and Captain M. Dyachenko was shot down'.[5]

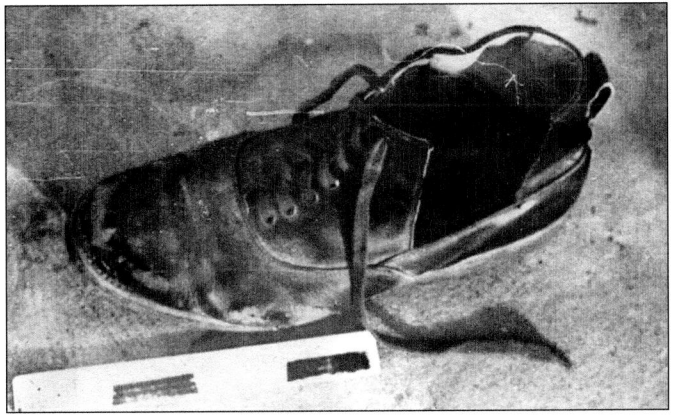

The shoe is the 'killer': the shoe that caused the fatal accident of technician P. Akulov.

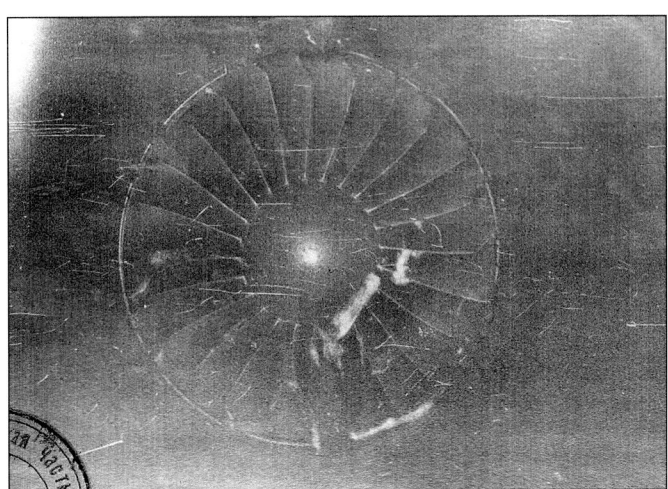

Damage to the first stage of the left engine compressor.

A view of the left lower section of the Su-25 Bort Number 10, with the intake of the left engine.

The investigation, undertaken by an independent investigator of the Air Force, Senior Lieutenant A. Anfimichev, established that the aircraft technician, Lieutenant Akulov, was on duty at the maintenance post and was carrying out an inspection of aircraft No. 10. At the same time, his boots were unlaced and the laces were dangling, preventing him from walking properly. After inspecting the right engine, Akulov went under the aircraft to the left engine, stepped on the untied shoelace, stumbled, fell into the danger zone of engine operation and was pulled into the air intake duct.

According to the deceased's fellow servicemen, he had proved himself to be an experienced, technically competent and disciplined professional during his service. He did not drink alcohol. Enemies and detractors among the staff of the squadron could not say the same. He had fully mastered the type of aircraft he was maintaining and had never violated safety measures before. He was well aware of the safety rules for operating engines. Before commencing the flights, he attended the mandatory briefing at the Regimental Engineer's Command Post (KPI) by the Senior Flight Engineer, Senior Lieutenant V.V. Podzolkov. Before he started flying he was instructed by Senior Flight Engineer, Senior Lieutenant Podzolkov, who read to him, on the record the *instructions to the technical post*.

As a result, the investigation concluded that Lieutenant Akulov died as a result of his own negligence in falling into the engine inlet of the aircraft and that there was no one responsible for his death. The criminal proceedings initiated by the garrison prosecutor's office into the death of the serviceman were terminated because there was no crime committed. But the question remains unanswered – how did it happen that such a disciplined man turned out to be so negligent with his shoes?

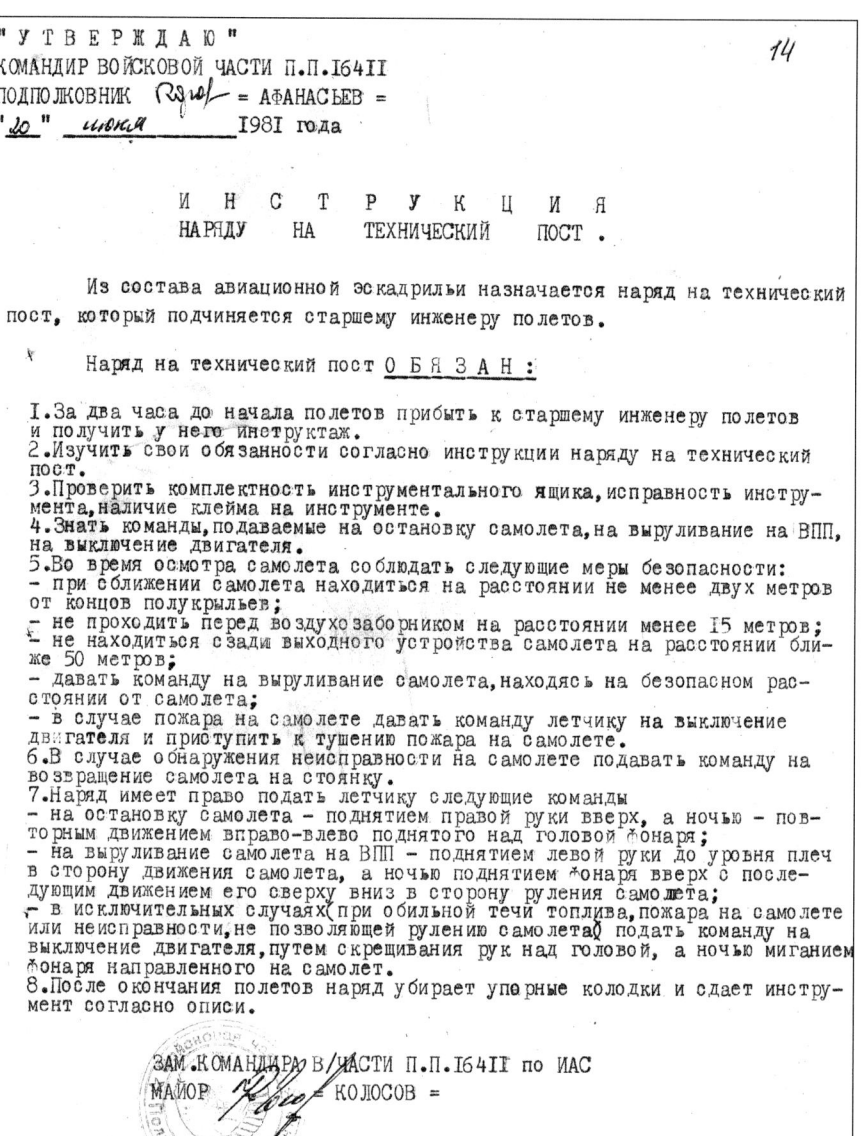

Instructions along with technical post.

Unfortunately, the squadron was also not without flying accidents. Almost six months after the beginning of combat operations, on 14 December 1981, there was an accident that claimed the life of the squadron's senior pilot, Captain M.E. Dyakov, in the first Su-25 to be lost during the war. While carrying out a diving bomb attack, the aircraft (construction number 25508101030) exceeded the permissible Mach number and began to roll on a glide path. Dyakov tried to recover the attack aircraft but loss of aileron efficiency and asymmetric separation of a 500kg bomb from one outermost pylon only, aggravated the situation. The aircraft collided with the mountainside. Investigation of the wreckage was hampered by the fact that soldiers 'dismantled' the aircraft's remains by deploying hand grenades.

After a detailed examination of the circumstances of the incident and the transcripts of the flight data recorder for operation of the Tester-UZ onboard systems, the initial version of a gunshot hit was not confirmed. It also turned out that, according to the planned flight schedule, Captain Dyakov was not supposed to fly that day as he was preparing to go on leave – his daughter had been born the day before. At the time, squadron commander Afanasyev was at a council of war at the 40th Army Headquarters in Kabul when he received the news of the pilot's death. This accident finally tipped the scales towards the decision to install BU-45A boosters in the transverse control channel of the aircraft.[6] In addition, a modification was made to ensure automatic paired emergency jettison of stores from outboard stations 2 and 10 or 3 and 9.[7]

Replacing Mikhail Dyakov, Senior Lieutenant S.V. Prichinenko was appointed Senior Pilot – Commander of the Parachute Department. Changes also occurred in the squadron's aviation equipment. To continue testing flights to try out the modes of the internal VPU-17A cannon and its effect on propulsion system stability, the prototype T8-6 (which had performed 20 flights during the 'examination') was returned to the USSR and its place in the last quartal of 1981 was taken by a new Su-25, Bort Number 12. The new aircraft and especially those involved in combat operations, always needed special oversight by the operator –

represented by the leadership of the military department, the developer, and the manufacturer. The combat effectiveness, reliability, survivability, and maintainability of the aircraft were all evaluated. In this context, the attack squadron had been repeatedly inspected by Air Force Commander Air Marshal P.S. Kutakhov and other representatives of the Air Force command. As always, such visits gave the aviators a lot of additional trouble.

As early as September 1981, Colonel General M.N. Mishuk, Deputy Minister of Aviation Industry M.P. Simonov, Acting Chief Designer Y.V. Ivashechkin and other specialists flew to Shindand on a four-day mission, together with the Air Forces Commander-in-Chief for Armament. The feedback, comments and suggestions, gathered during the meeting of the squadron personnel with industry representatives, enabled the further development of measures to eliminate the design and operational deficiencies identified during the 'special conditions' stage of military tests. These contributed to improving the reliability and survivability of the machine.

Next Phase

In December, the Su-25's 'Exam' combat test programme was completed and with the onset of 1982, the 200th OShAE embarked on full-scale combat operations. The intensity of sorties increased to four to six a day (sometimes as many as eight), resulting in an average of 178 hours flight time per Su-25 in its first eight months of operation in Afghanistan.

Technicians with the aircraft Bort Number 12.

A look under the wing of an aeroplane. Notable is the mixed armament installed on hardpoints, including (from left to right) a FAB-100 general-purpose bomb, B-8 pod for S-8 rockets calibre 80mm and another FAB-100.

A big operation sought destruction of a centre for the preparation of insurgent bands, as well as storehouses with arms and ammunition. This was carried out from 15 January until 19 January 1982 in the north of the country, in the area of Darzab. During the initial period, Soviet Aviation group forces made powerful bombing attack blows on the means of air defence, Islamist bands and strong holds of the opponent, before transitioning to aviation support. Altogether 72 sorties were performed with the consumption of 224 air bombs and 994 rockets. Two *zvenos* were involved in the operation. As a result, up to 950 insurgents, 500 small arms, four fuel depots, three supply depots, six pillboxes and four fortified settlements were destroyed. Three food depots, two radio stations, large quantities of small arms, ammunition and mines were captured.

From 16 May 1982, the fifth Panjshir operation was conducted in Kapisa province under command of the Chief of Staff of the 40th Army, Major General N.G. Tergrigoryants. It turned out to be one of the largest operations both in quantity of forces engaged and loss of equipment and personnel for the OKSVA. A total of 130 aircraft (including six Su-25s) were used to attack the heavily defended and fortified base of Ahmad Shah Massoud, whose group consisted of more than 30 armed formations numbering more than 5,000 men. Out of 108 involved aircraft, 83 percent suffered combat damage and four were irrecoverably lost. In turn, 5,370 insurgents, 203 emplacements, 120 DShKs and 25 mortars were destroyed. Captured trophies included 1,863 small arms with 24 DShK and five mortars. Personnel losses of the OKSVA amounted to 432 (including 92 casualties).

As the duration of the air units' stay in Afghanistan was limited by the command to one year, by the autumn the time for replacing the first 200 Squadron was approaching. After completing the flight training programme in the Soviet Union, the personnel of the second formation, headed by squadron commander's deputy, Major A.A. Kramarevsky, departed for Afghanistan in September 1982. In October, the third shift of the squadron, headed by Major P.V. Ruban, began training in Sital-Chai for later replacement of aviators in 1983. It should be noted that the rotation of aviators in the 200 Squadron began in the spring of 1982. First, the squadron's combat crew was replaced by Pyotr Popuchiyev and then, in the first half of June, Valery Arevkov and Nail Burkhanov arrived from Sital-Chai to replace them (instead of departed pilots Anatoli Korobkin and Yuri Roslyakov due to illness). In August, Lieutenant Colonel A.M. Afanasyev was replaced by Major V.N. Khanarin as commander of the 200th OShAE.

Outcome of the Combat Work

The 200th Independent Attack Squadron of the 40th Army Air Force, acting in the interests of ground forces, destroyed insurgent manpower and facilities. In the period from 19 June 1981 to 30 September 1982 the flying personnel of the first shift of the 200th OShAE completed more than 2,000 sorties, spent about 64,000 aerial bombs, and did not lose a single aircraft from enemy air defences' fire. The squadron's missions included strikes against planned targets and air support of ground forces (the main amount of combat work), as well as other tasks: reconnaissance, mining from the air, covering helicopter groups, et cetera. For exemplary performance of combat missions, the personnel of the squadron were awarded orders and medals of Afghanistan and the USSR, including the Order of the Red Star and the Order of the Red Banner.

The squadron's losses during the period were as follows:

- 3 personnel, of whom one was a pilot
- 1 Su-25 aircraft lost in an aircraft accident

CHAPTER 3
'TWO HUNDREDTHS' – SECOND SHIFT

In September 1982, the first change of personnel of the 200th Independent Attack Aviation Squadron took place in Shindand. On 8 September, the main group of personnel of the second shift, led by squadron commander Major Kramarevsky, in an IL-18, flew from Sital-Chai to Tashkent. On 10 September, the personnel of the new shift arrived in Shindand onboard an IL-18 flying from Tashkent to Kandahar then Shindand. The new replacements were put into operation according to the pattern already established in Afghanistan: ground training, tests, then 'flying through' – getting acquainted with the area of operations and the first strikes with the 'old-timers' as leading teams. Thereafter, they commenced independent combat work. The flying staff had qualifications of I or II Class – with the exception of two lieutenants who arrived in the DRA with qualifications of the III Class and passed the training programme in full (upon arrival at the new place of service). Major Vladimir Hanarin remained the squadron commander. The engineering staff under the direction of Major Naumkin, Deputy Squadron Commander for IAS, immediately began accepting aircraft, aircraft equipment and ground support equipment and the morning, provided flights which did not stop for a single day during the 'changeover' process.

More Action

The first major military operation, in which personnel of the new rotation of 200th OShAE took part, was the 'operation to destroy counterrevolutionary formations, to help establish and strengthen local governments, as well as to assist the local population in everyday peaceful activities'.[1] This was conducted from 5 to 15 October 1982 in Provincial Daghestan, according to the plan approved by the Defence Minister and by Soviet and Afghan troops under the command of the first deputy commander of the 40th Army, Major General V.G. Vinokurov. A well-armed group of mujahedin, totalling about 8,000 persons, concentrated in these areas. Opposition forces attempted to occupy key positions and found a major base in the centre of Afghanistan, thereby establishing their control in the area, intensifying anti-Soviet and anti-government propaganda and sabotage activities. Firing of small arms, mortars and rockets at government and military targets (including those of the Soviet troops) in the capital, became more frequent.

The combat operations consisted of successive blockades of areas around Kabul, air and artillery strikes on enemy groups, and subsequent clean-up of settlements, gorges and 'green zones' by units and divisions of OKSVA, DRA Armed Forces, the DRA State Security Service (HAD) and DRA Home Affairs bodies and troops (Tsarandoy).[2] At the same time, according to the reconnaissance data, air and artillery support was provided during the attack on insurgent concentrations, firing positions, ammunition and weapons depots, fortified settlements and caves. The 40th Army Air Force, along with a Su-25 formation of 200th OShAE, deployed eight MiG-21bis each from the 145th and 263rd Fighter Aviation Regiments (*istrebitel'nyy aviatsionnyy polk*, IAP), two An-26 and An-26RT aircraft from the 50th Independent Reconnaissance Squadron (*otdelnaya razvedyvatelnaya aviatsionnaya eskadrilya*, ORAE), a group of army aviation (Mi-8MT, Mi-24, Mi-8 helicopters) from the 50th Independent Helicopter Squadron (*otdelnaya vertoletnaya eskadrilya*, OVE), 335th OVE, 181st OVE and 262nd OVE each, totalling 66 machines. The aviation successfully coped with the assigned tasks.

The main method of combat operations in Afghanistan was, as before, air strikes on predetermined ground targets based on orders from the 40th Army Air Force headquarters. The orders included target coordinates, a brief description, force deployment, combat load, order of interaction, and time of the strike. A strike group (most often consisting of a Su-25 formation) of two attack aircraft formations were used for strikes against large insurgent targets. In large ground operations, more massive strikes were carried out by a squadron. A pair (or a platoon) of MiG-21bis from the 145th IAP from Ivano-Frankivsk usually constituted a counter-attack force against air defences. From June 1983, they were replaced by MiG-21bis from the 927th IAP from Bereza, Belarus.

Su-25 Bort Number 03 taxiing for take-off at Bagram airfield. Notable is the row of Su-17s (left side) and two MiG-21s in the background.

Sometimes helicopter gunship support involved Mi-24s. The force outfit included a target designation and search and rescue (SAR) team, usually a pair of Mi-8 helicopters. These sometimes flew with a local gunner who knew the terrain well, along with an interpreter escorted by scouts. When flying from Shindand AB, helicopter crews of the 302nd OVE, based at that airfield, were involved. Crews from other units were involved in operations from Kabul, Bagram and Kandahar airfields. Very frequent sorties were conducted in close support of ground and airborne units involved in ground operations, in conjunction with air gunners. In a smaller volume as compared to the first shift, solo search and strike missions against ground targets in assigned areas and ground reconnaissance flights, were flown. These sorties were usually performed in pairs at low and extremely low altitudes. During combat missions, the attack aircraft usually flew in pairs and formations. Sometimes, if necessary, flights were performed by a different formation but always in pairs.

Weapon Selection

In view of the limited combat radius of action of the Su-25, the flights were almost always performed with two 800-litre fuel tanks, two B-8 pods (20 unguided S-8 rockets of various versions each) and ammunition for the AO-17A gun (250 × 30mm rounds). The other options of loading were selected in accordance with operational orders, or the decision of the commanding staff of the squadron. Usually, it was two or four 250 or 500kg bombs – determined by the nature of the target. S-24 and S-24 heavy unguided rockets were also used, as well as all-purpose submunitions containers (KMGU). KMGUs were most often used for mine-deploying operations. These were flown by formations, with the leading pair equipped with KMGUs and the second pair usually positioned above the mined area and providing top cover. The mines were deployed from an altitude of 400m over the target area over a stretch of 2–2.5km in length. Often fighter escorts were assigned to provide cover. From the diary of the deputy commander of the 927th IAP, N. Karev:

> Two sorties. In one flight, two escorted Su-25s on mine-laying. The attack aircraft were crawling very slowly. In order not to get ahead of them we were flying in a serpentine pattern near them. Here mines, hundreds and hundreds of small green petals of anti-personnel mines started to fall from KMGU. How many of them have already been poured in three years? The mines detonate when they hit the ground and should self-destruct after a while. But not all were destroyed, and some remain. Therefore, there were casualties in the infantry from our own mines, scattered earlier. In general, such escorting is purely symbolic. You can't see fire from the ground from this height in the daytime anyway.[3]

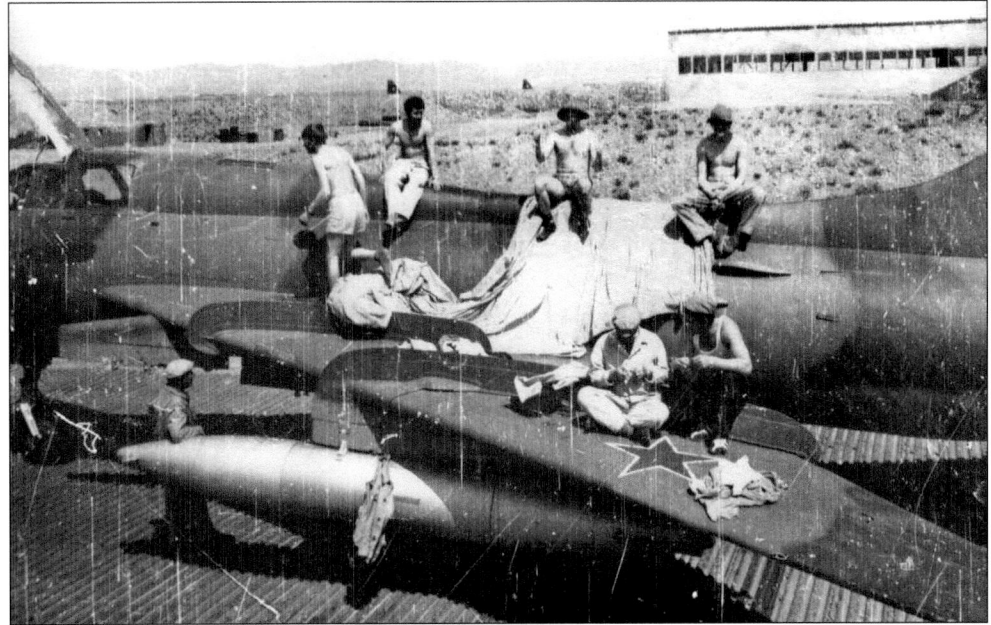

Work on one of two Su-17UM3 of the 200th OShAE, on the 'park day'.

As noted earlier, the situation in the Shindand zone of responsibility was relatively calm. The situation was tense in the south-eastern and eastern regions bordering Pakistan, particularly Parwan province, home to the influential local warlord Ahmad Shah Massoud who was a native of the area and highly regarded by the local population. Massoud had a heavily armed and well-equipped group under his command. The situation was further complicated by the fact that the densely populated Panjshir Gorge is isolated from the rest of Afghanistan to the north and south by difficult mountainous terrain. The only road in the gorge passes through Gulbahor and ends at Pasi Shahi Mardan. The Panjshir Valley was thus, a major insurgent leadership centre in key vital areas of Parwan and Kapisa provinces and also served as a training base and camp site, as well as a convenient transport corridor for supplying arms and ammunition via caravan routes from Pakistan. Despite a two-year truce with Massoud in 1982, the Soviets continued to fight in these areas against rival formations of Ahmad Shah.

In order to augment strike capabilities of aviation groups deployed in these regions, beginning in the autumn of 1982, 200th OShAE started operations from Bagram (Parwan province) and Kandahar (the same name province) airfields. One of the pilots serving at the time recalled:

Ahmad Shah Massoud (2 September 1953 – 9 September 2001) was an Afghan field commander, one of the leaders of the armed Afghan opposition Party the Islamic Society of Afghanistan, as well as its paramilitary wing Shurray-e-Nezor, and Minister of Defence of Afghanistan (1992–1996). He was also known by the nicknames Lion of Panjshir or Lakab, which means 'happy' in Arabic – and that already for leading an armed uprising int eh Panjshir Valley in 1975: the first armed insurgency of an Islamic opposition in the country. Massoud was ethnic Tajik, born in the village of Jagalak in the Panjshir Valley, north of Kabul into the family of Dost Mohamed Khan, who served as a Colonel of the Royal Police.

Afghan insurgent commander Ahmad Shah Massoud.

> As soon as any ground operations started in Panjshir, Pishgora, we were involved. As a rule, a *zveno* (four aircraft plus one spare) flew out. The missions varied in timing – sometimes a couple of days, sometimes a week, sometimes a little longer. We flew to Kandahar only once, somewhere in October – November 1982, for a week or two. For the rest of the time, we flew to Bagram almost every month until we were replaced. We used weapons available at local depots. We did not have to choose. Usually, the depots were completely emptied after our arrival. Often enough ammunition was brought to us directly from transport aircraft, bypassing the depot. We used everything – all kinds of bombs in calibre from 100 to 500kg, all types of unguided rockets (S-5, S-8, S-24, S-25), of course the cannon, and sometimes SPPU-22 pods. The S-5 was used quite a lot, more often than the S-8. Of bombs, we often loaded MBD multiple ejector racks with up to 32 FAB-100 bombs per aircraft (we called it 'hang grapes'). Targets were determined by the army headquarters. Planning the use of certain munitions was the responsibility of the squadron leadership except – except there were specific orders issued 'from above'.

Fuel Air Explosives

In 1983, in Afghanistan, the Soviets began deploying ODAB-500 bombs filled with fuel air explosives (FAE). The ODAB-500 was a variant of the high explosive aerial bomb and designed to engage manpower, industrial structures, lightweight engineering structures and to clear anti-personnel and anti-tank minefields behind folded terrain. The weapon was based on a volumetric explosion. On encountering an obstacle, a conventional explosive charge explodes. This destroys the thin-walled casing of the bomb, bringing the liquid explosive to a gaseous state and creating an aerosol cloud capable of penetrating into non-hermetic shelters (trenches, dugouts, et cetera). In 100–140 milliseconds, the initiating detonator in the capsule attached to the parachute, explodes and the fuel air mixture explodes. The main damaging factor of the ODAB-500 was the shock wave, which could reach an overpressure of about 3,000kPa (30kgf/cm). This wave had a long rarefaction zone (hence,

Su-25 Bort Number 03 in flight.

these are sometimes referred to as 'vacuum blasts') and proved very effective against enemy personnel. The radius of impact on enemy troops in open terrain was about 30 metres, while in field fortifications and trenches, it was 25 metres. In addition, the bomb ensured the destruction of open-topped vehicles within a radius of 30m.

The bombs were used only by personal order of the commander of the 40th Army Air Forces. They were brought by a special vehicle from the central depot, lifted up, and suspended from the aircraft. If the aircraft was on duty, the car with the containers waited at the airfield. If a flight was cancelled, the ODABs would be removed from the aircraft, packed in containers and taken back to the central depot. Beginning in 1984, ODABs were stored at the regimental general depot. The effectiveness of these bombs in Afghan conditions was not very high. The high elevation and heat in the mountains meant a lack of oxygen to sustain combustion, in addition to the mountain slopes and the wind in the gorges contributed to the dispersal of the gaseous cloud, which in turn changed the direction of the blast. On top of that, the main weakness of the boosters is that they have only one destructive factor – the shock wave – and do not provide any cumulative or fragmentation effect. Despite all these disadvantages, the vacuum bombs had a strong demoralising and intimidating effect on the enemy.

Deputy Squadron Commander Major A.A. Kramarevsky.

Shuttle Service

In July – August 1983, in the framework of routine operations conducted by forces of the 103rd Division VDV (*Vozusho-Desantnyye Voyska*, Airborne Troops) under the command of Major General A.E. Slyusar, in Kabul Province, the 200th Squadron performed the so-called 'shuttle' flights to mine the likely escape routes of insurgents in the vicinity of Kabul, to prevent them from leaving the combat area. At night, a ground group flew to Bagram. At dawn, the Su-25s, each flying in a section loaded with two PTB-800s and two KMGUs, would take off for Shindand, head for Kabul and carry out mining operations. At the end of the mission, they landed in Bagram as there was not enough fuel for the return leg. The planes were prepared (examined, refuelled, containers filled with mines) and then flew back to drop more mines. The pilots would land in Bagram, have lunch, refuel and equip, take off and go back to mine-laying again. They would return to Bagram, rest and refuel, take off and, at 6 or 7 p.m., would land at their base in Shindand.

Su-25 were also actively involved in the military operation, conducted from 8 to 19 August in Herat province by units and divisions of the 5th Motorised Rifle Division together with the DRA Armed Forces. During the operation, the identified groups of fighters in the green zone to the west and southwest of Herat received heavy air and artillery strikes. The blockade of the combat area hindered the insurgents' escape routes from this area and its subsequent combing was used to search for them, for warehouses with weapons and ammunition, as well as to filter out the local population to identify insurgents and their associates. In the morning, the Su-25s worked as a squad on assigned targets then flew on-call sorties during which, on approach, they contacted the Combat Control Group (CCG) and received new targets.

The enemy appreciated the Su-25's firepower. Judging by the western press of those years, sources connected with the insurgents acknowledged the high accuracy and efficiency of the attack aircraft and their ability to hit low-visibility targets in heavily rugged terrain. 'The distances from which they fired and hit targets suggest that the aircraft do not use guided munitions. New guidance and targeting systems may have been employed. In the biggest offensives, Frogfoot [western codename] aircraft have turned camouflaged fortifications into dust,[4] which were beyond their capacity a year ago. The aircraft strike the insurgents with more fear than any other weapon …'[5]

Deputy Squadron Commander Major Naumkin, in front of the Su-25 Bort Number 05, at Shindand AB.

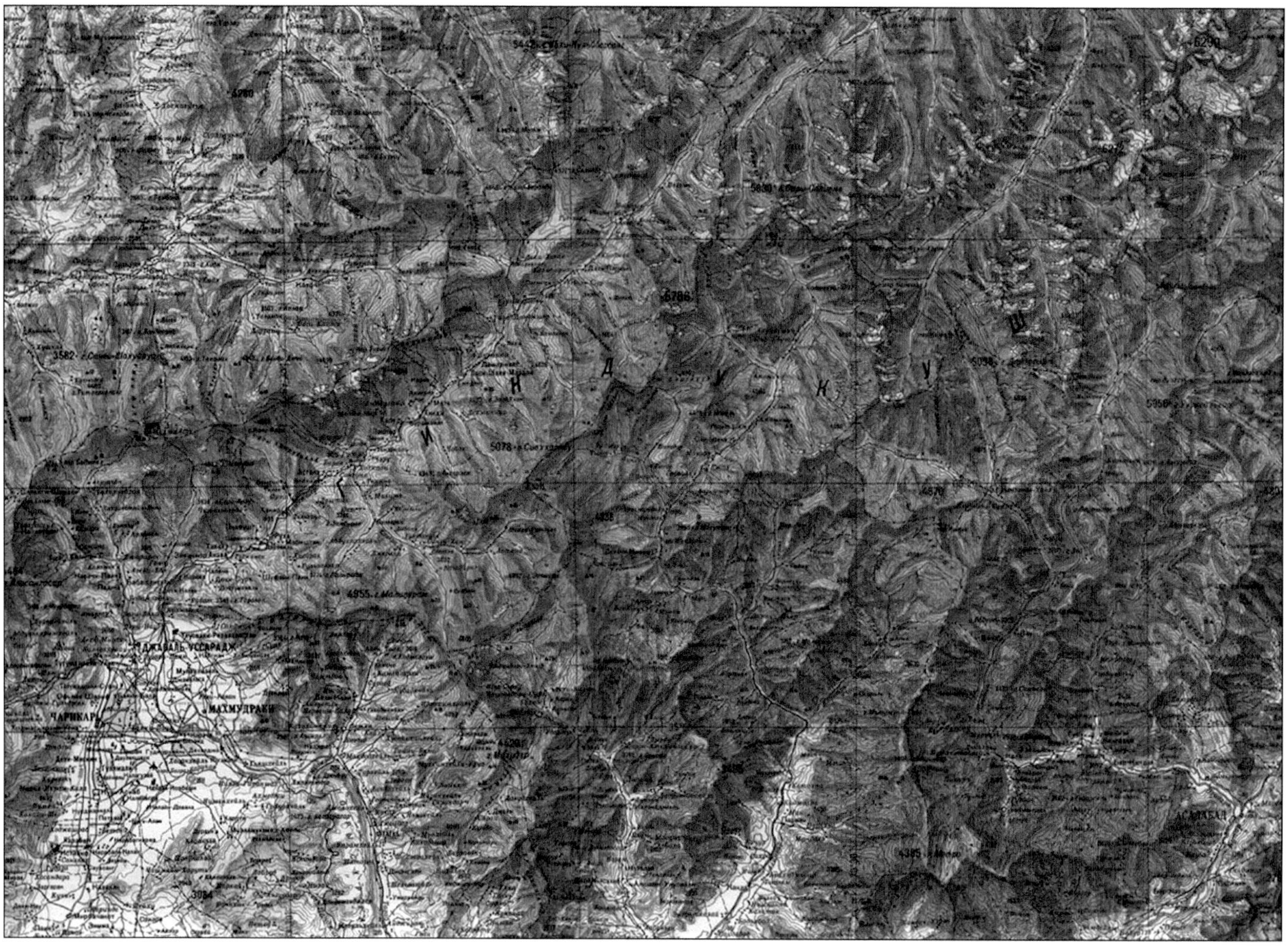

A Soviet map of the Panjshir Valley.

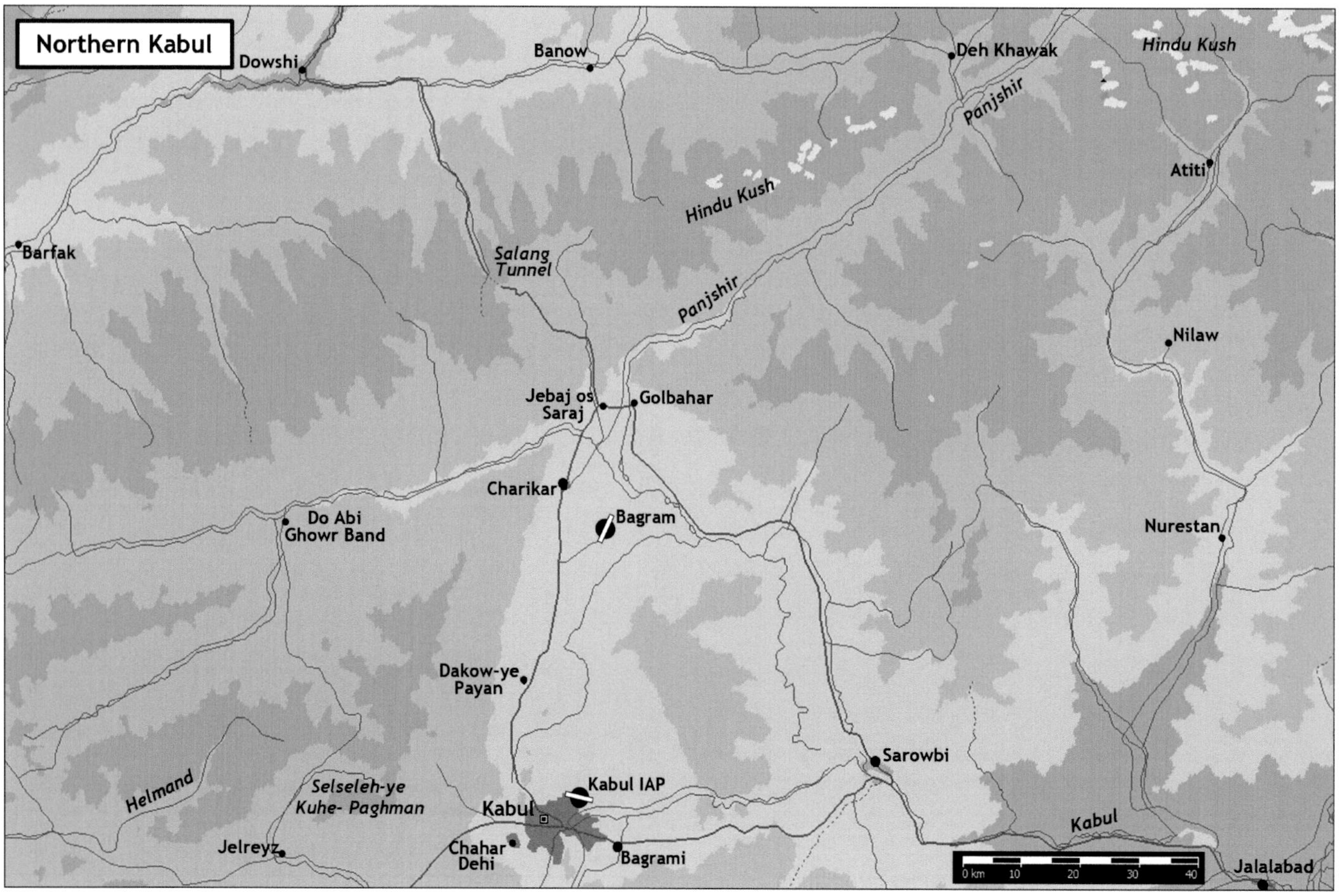

A simplified map of the area north of Kabul, with the Bagram AB and the Panjshir Valley. (Map by Tom Cooper)

In Shindand, the aircraft were housed in revetments close to the terminal. These hollows were somewhat narrow for the Su-25s, which could barely fit into them (they were originally built for aircraft with shorter wingspan, like MiG-21s and Sukhoi Su-7s). The aircraft had to be rolled into them very carefully so as not to damage the nacelles of the airbrakes on the wingtips. In summer it dawned at 4.00–4.30 a.m. and the maintenance staff rolled out the Su-25 and Su-17UM3 to the launch area an hour and a half before the start of flights, where the planes were unpacked and readied for take-off. They flew all daylight until 11.00 p.m. with virtually no night sorties. After finishing flights, the aircraft were inspected and prepared again and ammunition hung for the next day. After that, the aircraft were distributed back to the shelters. In winter, the daylight hours were shortened and flights had to be flown from 8:00 a.m. to 8.00 p.m.

Installation of two OFAB-250-270 bombs under the hardpoints of the aircraft.

Major Hanarin's squadron fought with the first line-up of aircraft. From a nominal strength of 12, no more than 10 Su-25s were fully mission capable at any time: failures occurred, aircraft sustained combat damage and due to a shortage of spare parts, one or two were almost constantly in the state of being disassembled and used as sources of spares. One attack aircraft in the squadron, according to recollections of the pilots and IAS specialists, was distinguished from the others by some 'features'.[6] When it was overloaded it could not be brought into a left turn – the aileron deflection was insufficient. In order to hold it straight, the pilot had to split the throttles to the right and 'strongly give the pedal'. All pilots were aware of the peculiarities of this wing and they performed the turn by first creating a roll, then switching to climb or, after switching to climb, reduced the g-force and increased the roll. No matter how hard they tried to level the plane, none of the adjustments gave any results – it remained 'crooked'. (Upon examination it turned out that its left-hand wing panel was longer than the right-hand one – peculiarities of the 'Georgian assembly' were an influence).[7]

The Su-25 was to be replaced as early as December 1981 by the aircraft factory in Tbilisi, with Captain Mikhail Dyakov initially planning to fly it. On 14 December 1982, Dyakov died in a plane crash. The acceptance team accompanied the coffin with the pilot's body to Tbilisi where they escorted him to his final destination on 19 December. The new attack aircraft (presumably number 14) was taken to Shindand by Captain V. Bondarenko, while the 'crooked' aircraft remained in the squadron. Incredibly, in the two years of flying in Afghanistan, that Su-25 aeroplane logged about 350 hours and never failed. Usually, normal planes were planned to be flown first and the 'defective' one, as a rule, was put in reserve. However, due to the large number of failures, it very often had to be released instead of the faulty ones. Eventually, in August 1983, the attack aircraft was handed over to the Air Forces State Research Institute where it was flown with four PTB-800s and transferred to Vladimirovka by Major Kulish.

Form No.1. Senior aircraft technician Dmitry Kechin and Head of Technical Department, Vladimir Kuzma, Shindand, August 1983.

The markings of combat missions (asterisks) appeared on the Su-25s during the first shift, tentatively at the beginning of 1982. They were stencilled in white paint on the left side under the cockpit canopy (behind the Bort number), five in a row. One asterisk stood for five combat missions. Replacement crewmembers used the rate of one star for 10 combat sorties, as the attack aircraft already had several rows of markings and as necessary, technicians added the required number of stars to their jets.

Aircraft Evolution

Damage assessment, repairs and recovery of aircraft were carried out promptly at the squadron's base and maintenance facilities. The timing depended on the nature of the damage and malfunctions and the availability of spare parts. The strength, reliability and simplicity of the attack aircraft design, as well as its good maintainability, proved helpful. For example, the aircraft construction number 25508101021, received in December 1981, suffered serious damage to the stabiliser, wiring, hydraulic system and made a hard landing. It was repaired and put into operation in early 1982, after a total of 340 hours of work by technicians.

The squadron personnel received enormous assistance in maintenance, repair and overhaul operations from the warranty team of the Dimitrov Aviation Plant in Tbilisi, which had been working in the DRA on a rotational basis for two years. By this time, in the course of intensive operation and combat missions, practically all the Su-25s had exceeded the laid-down warranty time limit (two years from the start of operation, or 225 flight hours), after which the plant's specialists were no longer obliged to service equipment out of warranty. Nevertheless, they continued to repair and refurbish the aircraft at night, side-by-side with the military. The squadron's IAS requests for piping, adapters, taps, sheet metal, angles, profiles, fasteners and other consumables were met fairly promptly by deliveries from the USSR. The factory provided the necessary units and spares directly from the factory in Tbilisi, writing them off as part of the warranty service. For their part, the squadron's engineers did not draw up and send claims reports of failures of warranty equipment, which threatened the aircraft factory with heavy fines. There may have been tacit agreements between the Air Force and IAP on this matter.

In 1982, the Su-25 attack aircraft began to undergo modifications based on damage bulletins.[8] The aeroplanes were flown to the Mary-2 AB, where the plant's team was based and a rework section was set up for the Su-25. When work on one aircraft was completed, the next one was brought from Shindand. Ready for handover, the aircraft was flown at the site and then flown back to the DRA. Revision of one Su-25 took on average of about a month. One of the jets was constantly undergoing modifications.

One cannot fail to note the large number of failures that occurred during the operation of the first series aircraft. The nose section equipment hatch covers and engine nacelle bonnets were equipped with lever-type locks that were convenient for technicians but insufficiently reliable, often spontaneously opening. Because of the weight of the bonnets and their semi-circular shape, when constantly opening and closing them, they became deformed which, in turn, along with the vibration of the aircraft from the firing of weapons and missile launches, led to their spontaneous opening in flight. The squadron had to fabricate homemade plates (the so-called 'paddles') and screw them onto the cowls and hatch covers.

When firing the cannon, the equipment mount in the forward compartment was torn from its mounts. Special weights had to be added in that compartment and plates were fitted on the gun carriage – both to reduce vibration.

A lot of the failures on the Su-25s were due to moisture ingress. Of course, the climate in Afghanistan is predominantly dry but it was terrifying to approach the aircraft after it had rained. The dampness in the wiring caused a short circuit in the firing pin: the cannon fired several times and bombs fell. It was enough just to switch on the aircraft's onboard power supply or lighting equipment. All this happened during ground checks.

The fuel tanks began to leak heavily – the wing tanks and especially tank no. 2 on which additional washers and elbows were placed and thus reinforced. The hatches of the wing tanks were insufficiently sealed, so additional rubber bands were subsequently fitted to their covers.

In the dry and dusty climate (Shindand was considered a tornado valley), the shock absorbers of the main landing gear legs failed. The sandy dust acted like sandpaper on the shock absorber 'mirror' (rod or oleo) and the loss of chrome resulted in leaks through the resulting abrasions.

The KT-163D wheels of the main landing gear mounts also caused many problems. Due to high temperatures, without forced cooling, they often overheated and 'spit out' the fuse plugs installed to prevent the tyre from bursting if the wheel drum overheated the air inside. This caused many peculiar problems. For example, when flying to Bagram, the crew of an An-26 did not manage to get there on time and before the Su-25. The ground crews at Baghram were not aware that the attack aircraft did not need APA-5 ground power unit to start, just the equipment necessary to cool the wheels.[9] There was a case when, during 'shuttle' flights, after performing a landing in Bagram, due to a hitch in the supply, aluminium rivets had to be removed from brake discs – and replaced – by a hammer.

Soviet Air Force units deployed in Afghanistan were always short on special tools and ground support equipment. For example, due to the shortage of APA-5s, engine starts were, in half the cases, autonomous from the aircraft's onboard batteries, which were available in sufficient quantity in stock and were simply replaced by new ones. There were difficulties in unloading and suspending the huge number of various sub-assemblies and weapons from the aircraft, as there was a shortage of cranes. While the smaller bombs could be uploaded and removed with the efforts of a few pairs of hands, the ammunition weighing more than 250kg was not easy to lift manually.

In the case of eight high explosive FAB-500s bombs, this operation was significantly delayed due to a lack of the required number of cranes. Airfield craftsmen built homemade trays, which were half bombs, stacked convexly upward in two long rows of 15–20 metres side-by-side. Using a crane, the bomb was lowered onto this tray and manually rolled to the very end of the tray, then the next one, et cetera. For the transportation of the ammunition to the aircraft, the trolley was brought to the end of the ground bays and the bombs were simply rolled manually from the bays to the trolley whose bays were on the same level as the homemade bays. As a result, one crane was sufficient to transport large numbers of bombs.

More Losses and Difficulties

Unfortunately, losses did not spare the second flight of the 200th OShAE either. On 11 April 1983, in Shindand, the squadron lost its second attack aircraft since the beginning of combat operations and again for reasons unrelated to enemy action. The aircraft, serial number 25508101021 (the same aircraft that was recovered from serious combat damage at the beginning of the year), under the command of the squadron's deputy commander for political affairs, Major A.N. Shatilov, crashed on take-off. With four OFAB-500s and full ammunition for the TLU (250 rounds), the aircraft, according to observers from the ground, strongly pitched up then began to yaw: as it climbed through 500 metres above the ground, it lost speed and then entered a dive at a critical angle of attack, followed by an uncontrollable descent. Shatilov ejected as the jet was 180 metres above the ground, leaving it to crash about 100 metres from the headquarters of the VDV division stationed near the airfield.

A crater about three metres in diameter formed at the site of the crash. The fuel that had leaked out ignited and the cannon's ammunition began to explode. Soon, a team of technicians led by First Lieutenant V.B. Kuzma, arrived and cordoned off the area where the attack aircraft had crashed. Kuzma recalled:

From left to right: Captain Borodkin, Aerospace Engineer, Captain Igor Lobanov, Aerospace Engineer, Captain Nikolay Styrov, Shindand, August 1983.

> When we arrived there, the situation was very serious. We did not know whether the fuses on the OFAB-500 were cocked or not. And then there were spectators from the division climbing into the thick of it and there was no way to cordon off the place. Then I managed to stop the column of five BMPs which surrounded the crash site and even fired several bursts of tracer over the heads of curious people to drive them away. The fuel was burnt out and the shells stopped bursting. They called in sappers who looked at them and said that they had to destroy them on the spot. But how could we detonate 2,000kg of bombs near the headquarters of the division? There will not be left a stone upon a stone! And then the armament engineer Pastushenko 'took a glass of alcohol to his chest', took out a special key, and went to the bombs. We went to a ditch (there was a ditch nearby). And so, he began unscrewing the fuses, turning his face away. When someone asked him later why he was doing this he answered: 'What if it blows up?' They gave him another glass of alcohol. He drank it and collapsed. They loaded him on the car and took him to sleep. The remains of the plane were evacuated. It was officially recorded that the loss of the aircraft was due to complete loss of the control power on take-off, due to combat damage received on the previous flight which could not be detected in time.

The harsh climate conditions tested not only equipment, but also people. The heat sometimes reached 55 degrees Celsius in the shade. The engineers and technicians had to protect their hands because they could not touch the hot metal without being instantly burnt. They worked with hand-made gloves, finding gloves and suitable rags wherever possible, as there was no special equipment. There was little uniform provision. At first, the norms of military supplies in the DRA were the same as in the Soviet Union. Technical overalls were sand-coloured for southern latitudes. The norm was one overall and two pairs of summer slippers for two years. But, in such climates and harsh working conditions their clothes and shoes would fall into disrepair much sooner. Nothing was left to do but patch the clothes by hand using available fabrics and even tarpaulin. The slippers which fell apart, were bound together with wire. Soldiers from the maintenance battalion of the air base made flip-flops for the summer from normal footwear: they cut off

Deputy Squadron Commander Anatoly Kramarevsky on Su-25 No. 04, with 17 stars for combat missions.

everything but the stripe across the foot and cut off the heel. Using half-woollen Soviet field uniforms in such climatic conditions was not possible at all. In 1983, the squadron was visited by a Commission for Logistics of the Ministry of Defence. The head of logistics from Moscow, seeing the officers, reprimanded them for their appearance. 'Ragamuffins!' After that, the standard was introduced – three full sets of 'technicians' for two years, and later four sets for two years.

Outcome of the Combat Work

In late summer 1983, the time came to replace the personnel of the squadron and it was the duty of the team led by Major Peter Vasilievich Ruban, to take over the international duty in Shindand.

From September 1982 to August 1983, the 200th Independent Attack Aviation Squadron of the 40th Army Air Force continued to provide air support to ground forces, airborne units and divisions of the Airborne Troops, carrying out bombing and assault strikes on concentrations of insurgents and infrastructure of anti-government armed formations. As a result, a large number of enemy troops, weapons and ammunition were destroyed. The personnel of the squadron were awarded orders and medals (including the Red Star Order and the Red Banner Order) for their courage, heroism, high tactical skills and fidelity to the military oath shown during the combat missions.

The squadron's losses during the period were:

- in personnel, 0
- in aeronautical equipment, one Su-25 aircraft lost as a result of an accident.

CHAPTER 4
THE ROOKS IN BAGRAM

At the end of August 1983, another rotation of the personnel of the 200th OShAE took place. Major P.V. Ruban's squadron arrived from Sital-Chai. The 80th Squadron was still the only regiment in the VVS armed with Su-25 attack aircraft and the replenishment and rotation of attack squadron personnel in Afghanistan was performed exclusively by this unit. The backbone of the new shift was formed by the pilots who took part in Soyuz-83, a large scale combined arms exercise conducted during early July 1983 in the Belorussian Military District under the leadership of USSR Defence Minister Marshal D.F. Ustinov. In accordance with the concept of the exercise, the regiment was tasked with redeploying at full strength from the Sital-Chai airfield to the operational airfield of Vitebsk. The Su-25 squadron then, with a full combat load, took off from the metal airfield at Idritsa and attacked targets at the Dretun training range, meeting the strict requirements set by the Defence Minister. Based on the results of the exercise, which assessed the feasibility of flying and fighting with an attack aircraft at a maximum combat load from a metal-coated runway, the actions of the personnel of the 80th Airborne Corps were awarded a 'good' rating.

From Sital-Chai, the replacements were transferred by an IL-76 transport to Tashkent. After spending the night at a transit point, they received their visas the next day, cleared customs and flew to Shindand. The baton transfer lasted for three days during which engineers and technicians, headed by the Deputy Squadron Commander for Aviation Engineering Service, Major Zapakhov, took over the aircraft, aircraft equipment and ground equipment from their predecessors. The flying personnel, under the watchful eye of their experienced comrades, were then introduced to the combat situation. As usual, flying was preceded by extensive ground training: they studied maps of the combat zone, received briefings, listened to the instructions of 'veterans', received weapons and equipped themselves. After completing the required minimum circumnavigation of the area, checks of piloting techniques, piloting and combat use with the flight control staff and squadron leaders of novices, the old-timers, wishing good luck to their compatriots, departed for the Union.[1] The rest of the squadron were put into action by their own forces.

Ruban's pilots began their combat work by searching for and destroying caravans, with a combat load of two UB-32-57 units and two PTB-800 drop tanks. On 19 September, near Herat, the full squadron (12 Su-25s) conducted a scheduled bombing attack operation. The convoy was planning to pass along the Herat-Kandahar highway and according to intelligence information, insurgents were preparing an ambush along the way. The combat order, received the day before, contained information about the intended location of the ambush, the appointed time of the strike, the required detachment of forces and data on the Central Command, radio communications and other details. They worked in a dispersed manner on the command of the commandant. The aviators accomplished their mission – the ambush was destroyed, ensuring the safe passage of the column. Later, when the squadron received information about the results of the strike, it was found that the pair that was closing it 'covered' a group of Dukh or 'spirits', numbering up to 12 people. For the pilots of this pair, this flight was the first combat flight.

At the beginning, the intensity of the squadron's combat sorties was not very high: flights in the morning until noon and in the afternoon, from 4 p.m. until evening. They had to take a break for a 'sleep hour' because of the unbearable heat and strong wind – the 'Afghan'. They were engaged in reconnaissance of caravans, direct air strikes against pre-set targets, mine clearance and direct air support of ground troops ('on-call'). The flying squadron operated in formation of standard and mixed flights in pairs: members of the headquarters section flew with all other pilots, depending on the tasks assigned but *zveno* leaders usually operated with the same group of pilots.

During September – October 1983, the 200's Su-25 took part in the operations conducted by units and sub-units of the 40th Army in the regions of Shindand, Farah, Bagram and Ghazni. They carried out bombing and rocket-strikes on identified insurgent groups, suppressing their firing positions and air defence facilities. From 12 to 30 October, the 1st Squadron operated from Bagram, from where it made eight missions, one of which was near Urgun. During one mission, they destroyed a group of 125 insurgents who had stopped to rest, for which the pilots of the squadron became the first to be awarded the Order of the Red Star.

New Jets

At this time, the first replacement of aircraft took place in the 200th OShAE. In September 1983, a team led by the headquarter section and the Head of the Technical Services Alexander Kozlov, went to the aircraft plant in Tbilisi to receive 14 new attack aircraft of the 4th Production Series. The first eight aircraft were about to be flown to Afghanistan when the command came to wait: by the end of the month the plant promised to prepare the remaining six. The officers took the advantage of a sudden 'holiday' and flew home to their families. They returned from Sital-Chai to Tbilisi with pilots who were to turn around the old aircraft and take them back to Mary, then receive the remaining six aircraft, together with ground support equipment and help transfer all of this to Mary AB. From there, Su-25s were transferred to Shindand, while their old mounts were returned from there to Mary. Some of the technical officers remained at Mary with the aim of handing over the old aircraft for so long that by the time their job was completed, the tour of the unit in Afghanistan was over and their comrades had already been replaced.

Like the aircraft of the first rotation of the 200th OShAE, the new Su-25s had an early camouflage paint job. Their Bort Numbers were from 01 to 14, applied in white outline only, below the cockpit. One of the aircraft (construction number 25508104026, issued on 30 September 1983) was given a Bort Number 13: in aviation (not only Russian, but also worldwide) the 'unlucky number' which the whole world associates with many different superstitions and omens, had a special attitude. In the Armed Forces of the USSR, flights on the 13th were practically never planned. If at all, the 13th day in every unit's calendar was a 'park and recreation day' which the staff received pay for. It was jokingly referred to as the 'Aviation Day'.

In the history of Soviet aviation, at different times in different units, there were planes with the Bort Number 13 in which some pilots flew with pleasure and some categorically did not want to. However, at the time of the events described, they tried not to tempt fate and aircraft: therefore, this Bort Number was never assigned. Perhaps, in part, it was due to the high accident rate that occurred in the combat units, with a fairly high intensity of training for the air staff. The reception of the Su-25 at the Tbilisi aircraft plant gave rise to some controversy when aircraft with the Bort Number 13 was received. Nevertheless, according to the reports of Sital-Chai pilots who were flying the new attack aircraft, it was the best of all they had flight-tested and thus the decision was taken to retain the number, although the 'warning bell' was rung all the time. Ironically, at the end of that aircraft's transfer flight, as it was taxing to its revetment, its tail light came off. Tragically, at the time, nobody was paying attention.

New Locations

From November 1983, tensions began to rise as the opposition units did not withdraw for the winter to Pakistan and Iran to rest, train and replenish their personnel, weapons and ammunition. Instead, they continued active combat operations within Afghanistan. The leaders of the Islamic League for the Liberation of Afghanistan were instructed to step up combat operations throughout the country, in particular to concentrate their forces in provinces bordering Pakistan, in order to capture major administrative centres. They also bolstered attacks along highways connecting crucial areas of the country, along pipelines, power lines and other important economic facilities, in order to disrupt regular cargo and logistics transportation. As a result, the intensity of hostilities increased significantly.

In late October, the squadron (under the command of air squadron commander, Major Ruban), redeployed to the airfield of Kunduz to take part in a joint operation. This was conducted from 28 October to 4 November by units and divisions of the 201st Motorised Rifle Division and the DRA Army in Kunduz and Baglan provinces. From the Kunduz airfield, ground attack aircraft conducted strikes on identified insurgent groups and targets in the mountain range 20–30km south-west of Kunduz, where, according to intelligence reports, ammunition and weapons caches of the Kunduz and Baghlan provinces' bands were massed. They also flew combat

Bagram AB as seen in the late 1980s.

Bagram airfield from a satellite.

The commander of a *zveno*, Captain N. Vdovin with a mechanic in a break between sorties, Bagram, February 1984.

missions in the areas of Tulukan and Faizabad. Georgy Kudinov, a pilot of the 200th OShAE, a Senior Lieutenant in 1983, recalled:

> In the annals of the 200 Independent Reconnaissance Squadron unit in 1983 there was such an episode – the redeployment of our unit (commander G. Chehov) from Shindand to Kunduz. The funny thing is that when we were tasked to redeploy we could not find any information about the Kunduz airfield. It was said that a helicopter regiment was stationed there, that there was a helipad, and no aircraft could land there. But the Su-25 should land. In general, nothing specific, no landing plan, no approach schemes, no radio communication data. You will understand on the spot. So, we got there as four crews, contacted radio control for the helicopter pilots, learnt something about the runway, overflew the runway, took a look, worked out the situation and landed. Then we talked to the helicopter pilots about conditions and ways of flying and began to work. It was there that our unit earned the nickname 'jewellers' – we attacked an arms depot in caves, destroyed the depot, killing just one sentry. What I remember from working in this northern region of Afghanistan was that the strikes lasted half an hour each. When the first round exploded, such a cloud of dust rose that it took a long time for it to settle. And I think that's where most of the shots were fired at us.

Nikolay Vasilievich Vdovin, a pilot of 200 OShAE, a Senior Lieutenant in 1983, complements Kudinov's memories:

> When we took off for the first time in pairs at 20-second intervals, after the first pair the dust rose to 30 metres, on take-off I saw only the edge of the strip and the nose of wingman Krylov, and my tail. Our Captain, Mr. Nazarov, dropped the receiver and thought we had been killed! Then I heard a whistle and tails came out of the dust cloud. Later the take-off interval was extended to two minutes because of dust. We flew up to three sorties a day and dropped all the bombs available in the depot of Kunduz: there was barely enough time to bring new ones by (Mil) Mi-6 helicopters. Then Ruban's *zveno* came to support us for about another week, after which we all returned to our base in Shindand. In Kunduz, we were assigned a permanent pair of ground spotters, and we worked well with them as a team.

In November and December, the 200th OShAE wing flew twice to the Bagram airfield for one to two weeks, from where the pilots worked in the Charikar Valley and Panjshir. The Bagram operation began in December. It should be noted that in November 1984, Captain Polovin, who was recalled to the Soviet Union due to certain circumstances, was replaced by Captain Chekhov who was appointed commander of the first line. Accordingly, Nikolai Vdovin became commander of the first tier.

In December, the squadron navigator, Captain Sharov, was sent to the Union to ferry four Su-25s of the first line-up of 200 OShAE aircraft from Mary airfield to Chirchik. According to Aleksey Nikolayevich's recollections;

> They were our planes from Shindand consisting of four units. In Mary where they were relocated from Shindand. Representatives of the Dimitrov Factory were going to do something with them. But then they said that there were no facilities in Mary and the aircraft had to be moved to Chirchik. Pyotr Vasilievich sent me to relocate them because, as far as I remember, only he and I were current on the type. I flew one aircraft before the New Year and the rest afterwards. The planes were in bad condition – all of them had some equipment failures, one of them even couldn't even retract the landing gear: I had to fly it like an An-2. I returned from this mission only at the end of January, during which time the squadron moved from Shindand to Bagram.

They all celebrated the new year together in Shindand and beginning 4 January, in one formation and later, as a full 200th OShAE, they flew to Bagram AB. This air base was located in the Parwan Province, 11 kilometres southeast of the town of Charikar and 47 kilometres north of Kabul, in a green valley bordered on three sides by high mountain ranges. Bagram AB was constructed by the USSR in 1961 as part of its technical assistance to Afghanistan. Located 1,450 metres above sea level, the 3,000-metre-long concrete runway allowed for simultaneous take off of a full squadron of combat aircraft.

Given the geographical conditions and locations of formations and units of the 40th Army and their assigned areas of combat operations, the 40th Army Air Force in Afghanistan was conventionally divided into four groups: 'North', 'Centre', 'South' and 'West'. Shindand was the airfield of West Group, which covered the western and southwestern provinces of Afghanistan (Badghis, Herat, Farah, and Helmand). Bagram, together with airfields at Kabul and Jalalabad, was the base for the Centre Group whose area of responsibility included the central and south-eastern parts of Afghanistan (south of the Hindu Kush mountain range up to the Pakistani border). Obviously, the redeployment of 200 Independent Reconnaissance Squadron to permanent bases from Shindand to Bagram airfield was due to the fact that this area was really 'hot' and strike capabilities of the air group 'Centre' was not enough. This was in contrast to the calmer areas in the area of responsibility of 'West' group, from the airfield based in Shindand. Hence, beginning from the summer of 1982, the Su-25 formation operated around Bagram almost permanently, flying mine-laying operations, strikes on assigned targets and close air support for ground troops.

Bagram, like Shindand, was an airfield shared by Soviet and Afghan aviation and was literally, full of aircraft: MiG-21, Mi-8, Mi-24, An-12 of the 40th Army Air Force and MiG-21, Su-22, Mi-8, Mi-24, An-26 of the DRA Air Force. During major operations (for example, in Panjshir), aviation equipment was forward deployed to other airfields (Kunduz, Ghazni, Kandahar, Shindand) – mainly Mi-8, Mi-24 and even Mi-6 helicopters. The air base accommodated aircraft hardstands, hangars for maintenance departments, a control tower (*kontrolno-Dispetcherskiy Punkt*, KDP) and a considerable number of other technical structures. In the northern part of the airfield (on the other side of the runway), in the area where the 345th Parachute Regiment was stationed, there were well-designed, hard-wall shelters for aircraft (said to have been built by the British), neat stone buildings equipped with two built-in rooms (pits) with earthen berms and concrete underground fuel tanks, cobbled or covered with metal slabs. There were 10 such shelters in total and from the moment the Limited Contingent of Soviet troops entered Afghanistan, all of them were occupied by paratroopers. Equipment was parked there and trophy weapons and ammunition were stored there.

The technical group, including newly-arrived replacements as seen at Shindand AB, in August 1983. Barely visible in the background right is the Su-25 Bort Number 09, with marks for combat sorties – white asterisks.

The squadron was housed in three modules: a flight crew module, an engineering module and a barracks module for conscripts. The air gunners lived in a separate room in the same module with the pilots.

The Su-25s were initially parked on the taxiway at the southern end of the runway, not far from the duty unit. This area had been used by the attack aircraft since their first tours to Bagram and remained assigned to them until the squadron 'moved' to the 'English' parking area in March 1984. As the apron was close to the runway, after taxi, the Su-25s immediately steered onto the runway and took off on a 30-degree course north-eastwards towards Panjshir. They landed on the same course, touched down, turned off the runway and rolled across the airfield to their parking spot, using the main taxiway. They had to work at the highest pace: take-off within 20 minutes (maximum 30) after receiving the task. Planes were prepared by everybody, even an elderly Chief of Staff was carrying ammunition, holding a briefcase with

Yu. Krylov, P. Ruban, A. Yakovlev, meeting for the New Year in Shindand.

Captain N. Lyubchik and Captain N. Prikhodko, Notably, the aircraft behind them was marked with asterisks for combat missions, Shindand, 1983.

Nikolai Prikhodko and Victor Rassokha, Shindand, 1983.

documents under one arm, while the other hand pulled a cart with S-25s, which was usually pulled by two to three people. On average, the tactical pilots conducted one to three sorties per day. The real 'record-breakers' were the pair, Lyubchik-Prykhodko, who flew five sorties per day, three times.

Adjustments

On 16 January 1984, in the midst of the Bagramskaya operation, the 200th Independent Attack Aviation Squadron suffered its first combat loss. A formation led by the unit commander, pilot Class I Major Peter Vasilievich Ruban and including Senior Lieutenant V. Rassokha, Captain N. Prikhodko, and Senior Lieutenant L. Sturov, attacked a fortification near Urgun. In the course of the attack, the Su-25 Bort Number 13 received damage from an automatic weapon on the right side, which resulted in a broken aileron control line. The aircraft fell into a spin and according to Ruban's wingman, Victor Rassokhi's report, Ruban tried to hold it level but then ejected when the jet rolled 90 degrees. His parachute did not have enough time to deploy. According to the recollections of other crews, the impact had such a force that even the heavy 30mm cannon of the jet 'bent into an arch' when hitting the slope of a mountain. The pilot was picked up by a crew of the 335th OVE and died on the way to hospital. Nikolay Vdovin recalled:

> At that time, we flew to the north as a unit. When we returned we saw from above that there were only three planes from Ruban's unit (they flew to Urgun), and we thought the fourth one was damaged and was towed to the maintenance station. After landing we learned that Ruban had been shot down by DShK fire. He was in a dive when flipping upside down and going straight in. The wingman pulled up in the last moment because of following him to a very low altitude: he did not see the moment of Ruban's ejection. The other pair (I do not remember who) saw it. As it was later calculated, Vasilievich did not have 1.2 seconds to open his parachute. He was found by a Mi-8, still alive, but all shattered: Pyotr Vasilievich died in the arms of our doctor (an Armenian, I do not remember his last name) on the way to the hospital. Ruban was not only a commander for me, but also a friend: we were family friends, and we visited his wife Tatiana every year in Tallinn. Two days before his death Pyotr was promoted to Lieutenant-Colonel, but he did not find out about it.

Ironically, on the day of Ruban's death, documents arrived at the headquarters granting him the rank of Lieutenant-Colonel. The Su-25 he flew, Bort Number 13 (don't believe the omens after that!) opened the account of that type's combat losses to enemy fire. That said, the personnel of the squadron under command of Ruban flew 1,149 sorties (or 1,119 hours) of combat over four months, delivering air strikes on the amassed rebels, arms depots and ammunition depots. As a result of combat and political training P.V. Ruban's squadron was named one of the best units in the Air Force of the limited contingent of Soviet troops in the DRA.

Unfortunately, the loss of the commander was not the only loss among the personnel of the squadron. Just within a day, on 18 January, an An-12 which was delivering ammunition to units of the Afghan Army, was shot down by the Mujahideen near Mazar-e-Sharif. Onboard the aircraft was the Deputy Commander of 200th OShAE.

After Ruban's death, Major Grigory Chekhov took command of the 200th Independent Attack Aviation Squadron. Captain Vladimir Lokhov became the new deputy, and Captain Georgy Kudinov was appointed commander instead. In March – April two pilots, Rustem Zagretdinov and Pyotr Shmonov, arrived from Sital-Chai to replenish the squadron personnel. At the same time, the Su-25 was nicknamed Grach, Russian for 'Rook', a gregarious Eurasian crow. The squadron commander, Grigory Alekseyevich Chekhov, signed the back of his cap with the initials 'Gr.A.Ch'. It was from that moment – not earlier and not later – that the attackers began to be called Rooks. Rooks also became the new call sign of the Su-25, replacing the previously used 'humpback' and 'comb'.

After relocating the 200th OShAE to the north end of the runway of Bagram AB – to the 'English' parking area – the aircraft were partially placed inside stone shelters with slots. At the time, the unit included 15 aircraft, including the two Su-17UM3s (still numbered 80 and 88) and these were occupying eight of 10

Ruban Peter Vasilyevich

Peter Vasilyevich Ruban was born on 11 June 1950 in the village of Hilchichi in the Seredyno-Budskiy district of Sumy region of the Ukrainian SSR. He was in the Soviet Army in 1970–1971. In 1972, he graduated from Chernihiv Higher Military School of Pilotry. He served in the Baltic Military District (321st APIB, Suurkul), in the Soviet troops in Germany; from July 1982, in the Transcaucasian Military District (80th Independent Squadron, Sital-Chai); and from the end of August 1983, as commander of 200th Independent Squadron in the limited contingent of Soviet troops in the DRA.

As a military pilot Class I, Ruban mastered the L-29, MiG-17, MiG-21, Su-17 and Su-25 with a total flight time of 1,765 hours. He completed 106 combat missions in the DRA, flying 96 hours. He personally led his squadron 30 times to destroy insurgent concentrations and firing points, destroying 14 DShK, three strong points, six cars, a fuel depot, two motorbikes, over 300 mines, three guns and about 250 insurgents. He was killed while carrying out a combat mission on 16 January 1984 and was buried in Zaporizhzhya city, the regional centre of the Zaporizhzhya region of Ukraine.

Lieutenant Colonel Ruban was awarded the Title of Hero of the Soviet Union (posthumously) by Decree of the Presidium of the Supreme Soviet of the USSR on 17 May 1984, for courage and heroism shown while rendering international assistance to the DRA. He was awarded with the Gold Star Medal, Order of Lenin, Order 'For Service to Motherland in the Armed Forces of the USSR', III degree, and other awards. Secondary school No. 62 in Zaporozhye and a supertrawler, which was built in Nikolaev, were named after P.V. Ruban, Hero of the Soviet Union. In the Room of Military Glory of the 378th Regiment, was a corner for the Hero of the Soviet Union P.V. Ruban. There was a competition among the pilots of the regiment for the right to fly for him.

The commander of the 200th OShAE, Major P. V. Ruban, with non-commissioned officers of his unit.

Captain V. Lokhov (left), Deputy Squadron Commander, and Major G. Chekhov (centre), commander of the 200th OShAE, Bagram, 1984.

R. Zagretdinov, V. Eliseev, and N. Prikhodko, Bagram, 1984.

Nikolay Vdovin recalled:

> Alekseich changed a lot when he became a plane commander, we all noticed that and it was under the influence of the burden of responsibility for all of us, he did not want to risk us. That is why we begged him for a fortnight to allow us to perform bombing raids from 600 metres with dive bombing. The first such mission we flew was against targets in the Jalalabad area. Jura Krylov was the first to dive-bomb. We blew up a 100x100m fortress, an ammunition warehouse. The second flight was made in front of everybody. The target was 7.5km from the airfield and everybody was watching from the ground. Again, we blew up the depot, after which Chekhov authorised these tactics and in two weeks, we had a score of seven ammunition depots. In May, Shemetov flew with a hole in his belly, caught in the zone of his own bomb splinters – either he could not keep the distance behind the leader or the bomb had a conventional fuse. From June onwards there was virtually no flying like this: the main task was to provide air support to the troops.

shelters: two were given to the maintenance crews. In addition, to accommodate aircraft, platforms made of metal decking were set up in the spaces between the trenches and at the end of the apron (both two-seaters were placed there). On a small platform between the shelters, there was a one-storey squadron headquarters building. The start-up position was in front of the apron: after the start, aircraft taxied to the northern end of the runway and took off on a southward course (210 degrees), landing on a reverse course (30 degrees). There was one occasion when they landed on the runway to the south with little fuel left and had to taxi across the airfield to their parking place on 'the last drops of paraffin'.

Hard at Work

Sometime later, the assault squadron participated in all major operations: Panjshir, Herat, as well as three consecutive Kabul operations. The Panjshir operation was the most ambitious in its concept, preparatory phase, duration and the number of forces and equipment involved. By April 1984 the grouping of the 'Panjshir master', Ahmad Shah Massoud, reached a strength of about 3,500 men. It had extended its sphere of influence beyond Panjshir by establishing itself in Khost-o-Fereng, Nahrin and southern Takhar provinces. Following an urgent request from the Afghan leadership, Moscow decided to conduct a large scale military operation (the seventh) in the Panjshir Gorge of Parwan Province with the aim of inflicting a decisive defeat on Ahmad Shah.

Ishmukhametov, head of the Technical Group, and A. Seregin, senior technician of the group, Bagram, summer 1984.

The operation was carefully and extensively prepared. It involved about 200 aircraft and 190 helicopters and more than 11,000 Soviet and 2,600 Afghan servicemen. The Air Force grouping was assembled in Bagram from all airfields. In addition to local MiG-21bis, 927th IAP, Su-17M3R of the 263rd APIB and Su-25 of the 200th OShAE, a squadron of Su-17M3 from the 156th APIB – all from Kandahar AB – and several squadrons of army aviation from Jalalabad, Kandahar and Kunduz were also added. Marshal S.L. Sokolov, First Deputy Minister of Defence of the USSR, and Lieutenant General L.E. Generalov, commander of the 40th Army, directed the operation. It started on the 19 April at 4.00 a.m. in the morning with a powerful air and artillery preparation. After two days of air strikes by Su-24 bombers and Su-17 fighter-bombers, flown from Soviet airfields, the troops entered the valley on 22 April without encountering any significant resistance. The operation was partly successful – the rebel infrastructure that had built up during the earlier truce, was destroyed and one of Massoud's comrades-in-arms, Abdul Wahed, was taken prisoner.

For aviation, the days of May 1984 were particularly stressful: during the Panjshir operation. The squadron flew up to 70 hours of combat flying in a month, or 150 sorties, which was equal to one year's flight time of the Soviet Union's. During air training, Su-25s, together with MiG-21s and Su-17s from Bagram, flew strikes on assigned targets, completing the treatment of sites after the work of bombers from the Union. During the main phase of the operation, the attack aircraft, together with Mi-24 attack helicopters, provided cover for the landing of troops: they constantly hovered in the air in pairs, replacing each other. For example, the pilot log-book of Nikolay Vdovin recorded 21 combat sorties during this period, of which nine were in support of troops in pairs and the rest of the strikes against ground targets by a group, mainly by the squadron-staff.

Ahmad Shah Massoud, having an extensive network of agents in Kabul, had received all information about the forthcoming operation 15 days before it was initiated. He removed most of his units and locals from harm's way, relocating them to the green zone of Charikar, Nijrab, Khost-o-Fereng and other districts in northern provinces of Afghanistan. It became clear that once the Soviets returned to their permanent bases, the Mujahideen would refresh their ranks in Pakistan and everything would begin anew. The widespread propaganda about their 'success' in the operation significantly strengthened Ahmad Shah's authority among the population and enabled him to expand his zones of influence in the northern part of the DRA. He created new base strongholds in the remote mountainous regions, established bases in the Hilau and Warsaj Gorges and subdued small groups of dushmans, including those from other Islamic movements.

Since aircraft always posed the greatest threat to the insurgents, the fight against aircraft and helicopters had been a high priority. Opposition units had anti-aircraft equipment which could hit air targets only at low altitudes: ZPU machine guns, Chinese-made DShKs, Swiss Oerlikon-Buhrle anti-aircraft guns, twin machine guns, as well as small arms (AK-47 rifles, Bur-type rifles, which had a high penetration and range)[2] and even RPGs.

Tactics for dealing with aerial targets consisted of firing at planes and helicopters as they took off, landed or when they attacked the target and descended to heights of 300–600 metres. This involved intense fire from all types of weapons, usually at the wingman in pairs, which reduced the possibility of detection and retaliation. For DShKs and ZPUs, trenches were usually constructed in the form of vertical shafts at dominating heights with a defined firing sector, which were carefully camouflaged. DShKs were also equipped with open positions – often concrete, with special gaps for concealment of personnel – designed to fire at both air and ground targets. The insurgents used DShKs, mortars, mobile rocket launchers (on jeep chassis) and 76mm rocket launchers to destroy aircraft at the airfields. Thus, on 11 May 1984, during the night firing at Bagram airfield, four MiG-21bis of the 927th IAP on duty were destroyed and an enlisted soldier was killed in the fire. The fire nearly spilled over to the reconnaissance camp, but the aircraft, some of which were already covered in smoke, were removed in time.

In spite of a significant number of anti-aircraft weapons, the insurgents' air defence efficiency remained low due to their lack of medium and high altitude weapons. However, since the spring of 1984, the enemy's air defences began to increase. In addition to the low altitude ones, the bandit formations began to receive modern anti-aircraft weapons – man-portable air defence systems (MANPADS) of American production, the General Dynamics FIM-43A 'Red-eye' with an infra-red homing head, British Short Brothers 'Blowpipe', as well as Chinese-made MANPADS 'Arrow-2M'. Their total numbers by 20 April 1984 reached 47.

MANPADS training courses were held in air defence training centres in Pakistan under the guidance of American and British advisers-instructors. The use of MANPADS against attack aircraft, began in March with about 20 firings (all missing) and a total of 62 MANPAD launches were recorded during the year. All of the squadron's personnel subsequently accomplished all of their combat missions without casualties.

From combat sorties, the Su-25s suffered damage from small arms and small calibre anti-aircraft fire, at times quite serious. For example, on one of the sorties, Sergey Shemetov's plane (he worked in two formations and was in the tail pair) suffered damage to its left engine and had to land on one of them. During examination on the ground, a core from a DShK bullet was found.

In another case, six aircraft worked in the Urgun area: the pair of the squadron commander, Captain Sharov and the wingman of Captain Vdovin. The aircraft was hit in the right wing from DShK, damaging the aileron link. At the moment of the hit, the aircraft was in a shallow right roll, turning towards the target. After exiting the dive with a left turn, the pilot managed to parry the roll with difficulty, launched all remaining S-25s over the mountains to lighten the damaged aircraft and slowly (in what is called a 'pancake'), made his way home.

In the same sortie, on the Su-25 of Victor Rassokha, a burst from DShK blew out the left wing panel and short-circuited the wiring, which resulted in all weapons dropping except one bomb. However, the pilot also managed to bring the damaged aircraft to his base and landed safely. The

Alexey Seregin, Bagram, at the height of the Panjshir operation.

holes in the fuselage and wing plating were patched and the damaged units and sub-assemblies were replaced. By the time they were fixed there were so many patches and it had such a 'combat' look, the aircraft could not fail to impress replacement personnel. In the case of the Vdovin and Rassokhi aircraft, the wing panels had to be replaced as a whole and the Vdovin's Chief of Mechanical Department, Slesarchuk flew to the Tbilisi plant where the panels were fully assembled and painted.

It's Technical

The attack aircraft of the second batch did not differ in appearance from the vehicles of the first. They had the same paint scheme and numbers, with no distinguishing marks – with the exception of marks for combat missions. The technicians of Chekhov's

Nikolai Vdovin at the staff house, Bagram, summer 1984.

squadron kept up the tradition of their predecessors and also applied white stars (one for 10 sorties) on their aircraft using the same stencils and in the same places on the left side of the cockpit, under the canopy.

Apart from combat damage, there were various aircraft failures. The 01 series aircraft, inherited from its predecessors, had several cases where the bombs failed to separate. Once, a Su-25 landed with four FAB-500s – all under the right wing only. Similar failures occurred on the aircraft of the 4th Series, prompting the decision to change the usual weapons configuration in the following fashion: UB-32-57s or B-8s at the outer stations (2 and 10), followed by PTB-800s at stations 3 and 9 and 250–500kg bombs at the inner stations (4, 8 and 5, 7). In the case of a failure to release bombs, the roll torque was less and release of the bombs could be one at a time because the 4th Series had a system installed that prevented unpaired dumping of stores from stations 2 and 10 and 3 and 9.

In addition, there were cases of incomplete expansion of the separation pistons, those of pistons firing while the aircraft was on the runway; destructions of the front wheel mounting bolts after landing due to exceeding side wind speed limits (13m/s); and failures of drop tanks due to destruction of the gaskets.[3] Failures of instrumentation and sighting equipment were considered a trifle. Duplicate instruments were used and sighting in manual mode could be accomplished – sighting conditions for automatic and manual modes were calculated before departure.

Routine maintenance of the aircraft and the repair of combat damage were all performed by the squadron's Maintenance Department. As in previous rotations, the squadron was supported by constant presence of the factory's team responsible for warranty service – which usually eliminated deficiencies, but also design and manufacturing effects without bigger problems. Aircraft were used evenly and thus, the equipment spared. This personnel had been absent since the start of the fourth rotation – and sorely missed: before soon, the unit's technical personnel were tired. They stood on constant duty, by day and night, with at least a *zveno* of Su-25s – always supported by ground personnel – always on duty. There was very little respite and breaks, if taking place at all, were possible only during lunchtime, on afternoons or early morning hours. These were issues that were only gradually solved, foremost through extending the breaks.

In September, the one year assignment to Afghanistan expired and the personnel of Chekhov's squadron was to be replaced. Meanwhile, the formation of new Su-25 regiments in the VVS was in full swing and the Dimitrov aviation plant in Tbilisi was ramping up production of attack aircraft: 62 aircraft were produced in 1984. A year earlier in 1983, the Air Force of the Odessa Military District at the airfield of Artsis had begun reconfiguration and retraining of the Su-15-equipped 90th IAP,[4] thereby becoming the second formation (after the 80th OShAE) to be expanded into a bigger formation. In summer 1984, two western military regions (the Belorussian and Pre-carpathian) began to form ground attack aviation regiments: the 357th Squadron at the Pruzhany AB, and the 368th Squadron at the Zhovtneve AB.

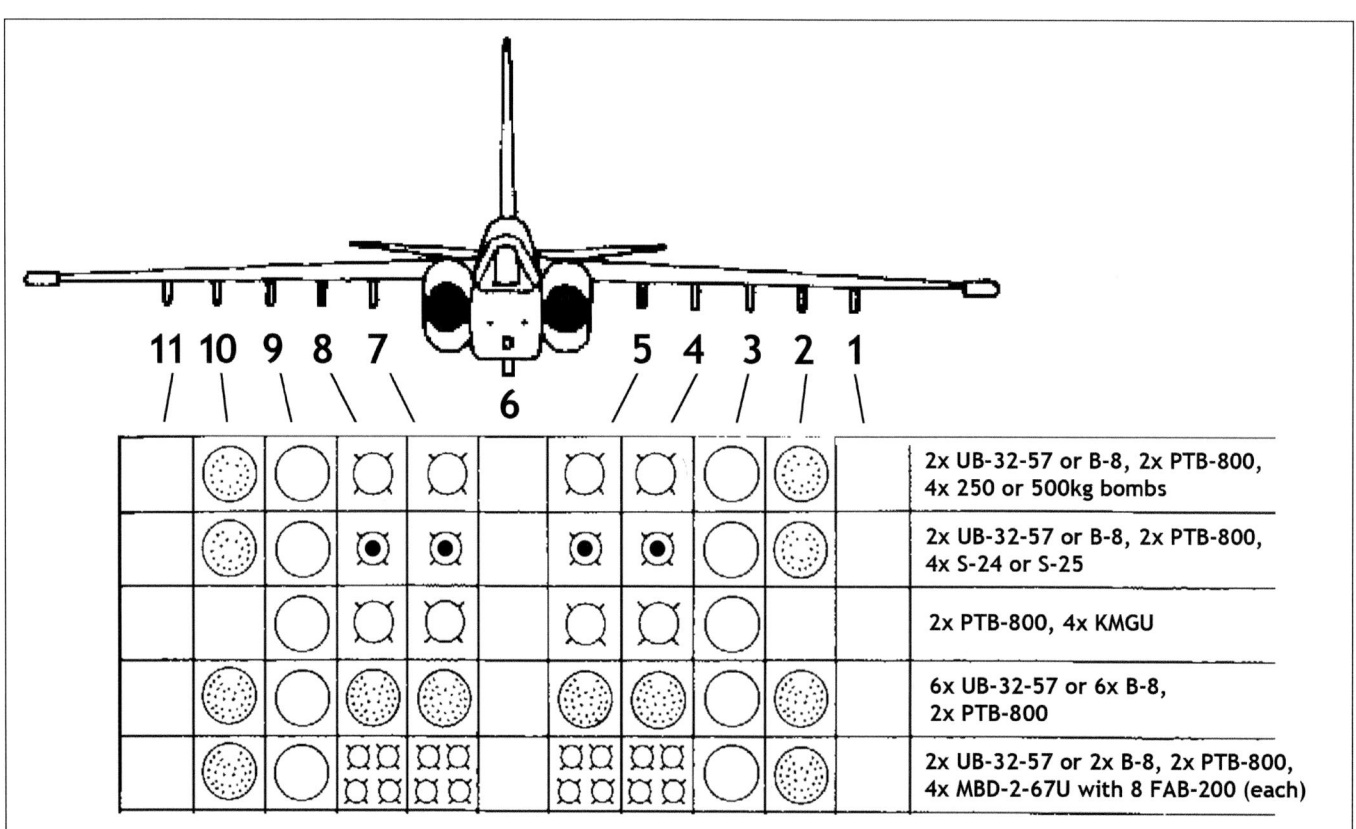

A diagram denoting stations on the Su-25 and the most frequently used weapons configuration (other configurations were theoretically possible but not used for reasons described in the text). Notably, while stations 1 and 11 were rated and wired for installation of lighter weapons – like R-60 short-range, infra-red homing, air-to-air missiles, useful for self-defence purposes against enemy interceptors – in Afghanistan 1981–1985, these were unnecessary and never used. In similar fashion, the centreline station under the fuselage – Station 6 – was never used. (Diagram by Tom Cooper)

Outcome of the Combat Work

From 26 August 1983 to 26 September 1984, the personnel of the 200th OShAE of the 40th Army Air Force conducted about 6,500 combat sorties. Its personnel was awarded the Order of the Red Star and the Red Banner medals 'For services in combat' and 'Warrior-Internationalist from the grateful Afghan people' for their courage, heroism and high level of training displayed in the performance of combat missions.

The squadron's combat losses during the period were:

- in personnel, two officers of whom one was a pilot
- in aeronautical engineering, one Su-25 aircraft

From left to right: pilots A. Yakovlev, G. Chekhov, N. Lyubchik, N. Prikhodko, Y. Krylov, V. Lohov, G. Kudinov, S. Gorokhov, and N. Vdovin, Bagram, summer 1984.

CHAPTER 5
FROM SQUADRON TO REGIMENT

In September 1984, in accordance with the 'Relay' programme for personnel rotation of aviation units in the DRA, another, third rotation of the personnel of the 200th OShAE took place. This time the first squadron of the 90th Independent Attack Aviation Regiment of the Air Force of Odessa Military District, commanded by Lieutenant Colonel N.V. Shapovalov, was sent to Afghanistan. This was only the second unit (after the 80th OShAE) to receive the Su-25 and the regiment was previously a fighter unit of the Air Defence Force equipped with Sukhoi Su-15 interceptors.

New Breed

The reorganisation of the 90th Fighter Aviation Regiment began in 1983. In March, the first group of its pilots, headed by Colonel V.I. Myakenkiy (senior pilot-inspector of the combat training department of the Air Force of the Odessa Military District), departed to Lipetsk for theoretical retraining on the new equipment. The group included: Deputy Regimental Commander Lieutenant Colonel A.I. Davydov, commander of the first air squadron Major N.V. Shapovalov, and pilots Bulakhov, B.V. Zholobov, T.A. Kononenko, A.V. Fonotov, S.B. Kharchenko, and L. Chernov. The next day, upon arrival and accommodation, the trainees began their studies.

The schedule was as follows: two pairs before lunch on weekdays,[1] one pair after lunch and an hour and a half of self-study; on Saturday, classes until lunch; Sunday was a day off. A set of disciplines – standard for retraining on a new type of aircraft; aircraft and engine, aircraft equipment, radio equipment, weapons system, aerodynamics, piloting, combat use and rescue equipment. The main emphasis was on aeronautical guidance, the weapon system and combat employment of the attack aircraft. The centre

The fourth shift of 200th OShAE, Chirchik, September 1984. Bottom row from left to right: I. Chmil, A. Porublev, N. Shapovalov, B. Zholobov, and A. Karpushin. Middle row: Y. Zubkov, A. Phonotov, V. Malyshev, S. Shumikhin, E. Pekshev, and V. Anyuk. Top row: V. Zazdravnov, S. Malookiy, N. Grushin, F. Ibragimov, T. Kononenko, V. Butorin, and A. Kolyako.

> The unit with Field Post Number 64298 was formed on the basis of General Staff Directive No. ORG/6/463856 of 18 April 1955 at the Sarata AB in the Odessa region in the period from 1 September to 28 November 1955 although the order of the Ministry of Defence set the Unit's Day as 27 November 1955. The regiment was designated the 90th Fighter Aviation Regiment and was organizationally, a part of Odessa Air Defence Corps, which was transformed into the 21st Division of 8th Separate Air Defence Army on 15 May 1961. On 29 April 1959, the regiment was awarded the Red Banner and a Letter of Commendation. Since 5 May 1960 the 90th IAP was stationed at the Artsiz AB (Chervonoglinskaya). In February 1980, 90 IAP was re-assigned to the Air Force of Odessa Military District and in 1984 transformed into 90th Detached Attack Aviation Regiment and re-equipped with Su-25s. Prior to that, the regiment operated following aircraft types: MiG-15bis (1956), Sukhoi Su-9 (1960), Yakovlev Yak-25M (1960), Yak-28P (1965), and Su-15TM.

was only just beginning to work with the Su-25, so training manuals specific to that type aircraft were few but used extensively for retraining on the Su-17M3 as regards aeronautical equipment, aeronautical armament and piloting. There were well-equipped classrooms with diagrams and mock-ups on these subjects. For example, the Zvedza K-36L ejection seat was studied on a K-36DM mock-up. Having successfully completed the course and passed all the tests, the group of flying personnel returned home. Meanwhile, in Tbilisi, the regiment's first group of engineering staff were completing their theoretical retraining on the Su-25 and preparing to receive their first batch of attack aircraft.

By order of the Air Force Commander, 16 graduates of Chkalov Borysoglebsk Military High School of 1983 were assigned to the Commander of the Air Force of the Odessa Military District. The young lieutenants dreamed of flying supersonic fighter-bombers MiG-27 or Su-17M3. The freshmen knew very little about the new plane and even less so from the words of the military instructors, such as subsonic, leaky cabin, mediocre aerodynamics and 'crude' design. Theoretical retraining of pilots fresh from advanced jet training was also held in Lipetsk, where the future attack aircraft pilots were constantly being jeered at by their colleagues, calling them 'tractor drivers'. However, as soon as the pilots had a chance to see the plane with their own eyes and get into its cockpit, their attitude to the stocky, ugly-looking machine changed.

The personnel were to learn the Su-25 by practice directly in the regiment. At that time, the airfield at Arciz was closed for runway repairs, as a result of which the aviation regiment was temporarily relocated to an airfield in Tiraspol and taken off combat duty in the air defence system (it still had the Su-15). The first 12 Su-25s were taken from the factory airfield Veli to the airfield in Tiraspol by pilots of the 80th Brigade.

The regiment's first flights with the Su-25 took place on 18 August 1983. The new aircraft were initially flown by the first squadron commander, Major V.N. Shapovalov and deputy commander of the first squadron, Captain A.F. Porublev. In the process of practical mastery of the new aircraft, problems of various nature, often leading to aircraft failures, arose. This included both piloting techniques and a purely psychological factor. Many pilots could not come to terms with the fact that they had to change from supersonic all-weather interceptors to subsonic battlefield aircraft and were transferred to the air defence units to their usual Su-15s.

Piloting the attack aircraft revealed other difficulties. On the glide path, pilots often did not maintain a given speed and altitude of the flight, touched down with a roll (small base and the track of the landing gear led to the subsequent swing) which, combined with the side wind, aggravated the situation. Progressive 'wobble' on the runway occurred and disproportionate effort on the pedals, when attempting to parry the sway, resulted in the nacelles of the airbrakes touching the runway. It was not uncommon for the aircraft to roll out onto the dirt and suffer the inevitable breakdowns. New fighter pilots also had to get used to pedal braking on the runways – improper braking often resulted in the wheels burning out immediately. The above factors combined to give rise to abnormal situations, mainly on landing and less frequently on take-off.

During the first month of flying, the regiment damaged six Su-25s out of an available 12. Aircraft with Bort Number 06 rolled out onto the dirt and broke the front strut. According to preliminary estimates, it could not be repaired: nevertheless, it was sent back to the plant. The unexpectedly high accident rate gave rise to rumours of sabotage among personnel unwilling to master the attack aircraft. To be fair, it should be noted that similar aspects took place during the mastering of the Su-25 in the leading 80th OShAE, but to a much lesser extent. Many officers in the 80th had voluntarily transferred from supersonic frontline aircraft – some wanted to change duty station and so filed reports of their transfer to a garrison near the Caspian Sea, others deliberately sought to master the new attack aircraft. The regiment had a different approach to the process of retraining on the Su-25 – the programme was personally supervised by Air Marshal A.N. Kutakhov. There were a few runway incidents but in the period between 1981 and 1983, they were few and far between and there was not a single instance of a serious breakdown of the Su-25 during training flights. The interceptors and attack aircraft were flying simultaneously at Tiraspol until the autumn of 1983. At the end of the year, the regiment transferred the Su-25s to Artsiz (the two damaged aircraft were transported by ground) and all the remaining Su-15s were transferred to other units.

In January 1984, the second group of pilots headed by Lieutenant Colonel V. Chergentsov, deputy commander of the 2nd air regiment for flight training, went to Lipetsk for retraining. After their return in February, Lieutenant Colonel S.V. Glukhov's third squadron left for Lipetsk. There is a 'story' about an incident that occurred in the third air squadron during the initial period of mastering the attack aircraft. Mindful of the results of the regiment's first flights on the Su-25, Glukhov, commander of the 'youth squadron', made an unusual suggestion to his subordinates. The squadron commander allegedly said that if none of the pilots would depart the runway during take-off or landing and break the plane, the commander would give his unit a box of cognac. In the end, all 16 lieutenants, yesterday's graduates, flew solo without incident.

Lieutenant Colonel Shapovalov's squadron was preparing intensively for a mission to Afghanistan. The flying staff

ROOKS IN AFGHANISTAN VOLUME 1

A Su-25 Bort Number 03 of the 200th OShAE, as operated from the Shindand AB in 1983. (Artwork by Yuriy Tsepurkaev)

Su-25 Bort Number 34 (construction number 25508106041), in which Senior Lieutenant T.A. Kononenko crash-landed on the Mazar-i-Sharif airfield, on 4 August 1985. (Artwork by Yuriy Tsepurkaev)

A Su-25 Bort Number 24 at the parking lot of the Sital-Chai AB.

The Su-25 Bort Number 26 (construction number 25508107070), issued to the VVS on 23 August 1985. As usual, this jet had already received its four-colour disruptive camouflage pattern already in Tbilisi. The same was valid for its Bort number, applied in form of a white outline only. The national insignia was applied in six positions: left and right side of the fin, top and bottom of all wing surfaces. Notable on the left inset is the 'Rook' insignia, designed by Igor Ryabchenko, a technician of the 378th Regiment's 1st Squadron. Notably, this jet received ASO-2VM chaff and flare dispensers atop the rear section of engine nacelles. (Artwork by Yuriy Tsepurkaev)

The Su-25 Bort Number 06 (construction number 25508109079) was issued to the VVS on 31 March 1987 and served with the 378th OShAP in Bagram as of 1988. It received the disruptive camouflage pattern No. 2, in mountain-desert-style, consisting of dark sand and dark brown on upper surfaces and sides, with some olive green on the top centre of the fuselage and engine nacelles. Bort number (also applied in Tbilisi) was in red, outlined in black and repeated in red on the drop tank, while the Rook insignia was applied on the left intake only, and – in this case – on a white shield outlined in yellow. (Artwork by Yuriy Tsepurkaev)

The Su-25 Bort Number 27 (construction number 25508110018), issued to the VVS on 30 June 1987 and as seen while serving with the 378th OShAP at Bagram AB, in 1987. This aircraft was unusual in so far as it received the mirror form of a disruptive camouflage pattern No. 5, which consisted of only two colours on its top surfaces and sides: dark sand and dark olive green (of which the latter had a strong brownish touch). Like on all the Su-25s manufactured in the 1980s, undersides were painted in the Soviet version of the BS381/697 light admiralty grey colour. As standard by the time, the Bort number was applied in red with black outline and repeated on drop tanks in white. (Artwork by Yuriy Tsepurkaev)

The Su-25 Bort Number 50 (construction number 25508110071), issued to the VVS on 30 September 1987. This jet served with the 2nd Squadron of the 378th OShAE at the Shindand AB, in 1988. It was painted at the factory in Tbilisi in the disruptive camouflage pattern No. 3, known as the 'mountain-desert', consisting of dark sand, dark brown and (along upper surfaces of the centre fuselage and engine nacelles) dark green on top surfaces and sides. 'Personal insignia' shows a rook clutching the S-24 unguided rocket while spitting. The Islamic Committee was applied on the left side of the forward fuselage only, whilst seven of the eight red stars, denoting the number of combat missions, had the digit '50' stencilled in the centre. (Artwork by Yuriy Tsepurkaev)

The original emblem of the Rook attack aircraft.

A Su-25 loaded with bombs and PTB-800 drop tanks en route to the target, as seen from the wingman's cockpit.

Pilots of the 2nd Squadron, 378th OShAE, Bagram, June 1985. Rear row: A. Kolyako, S. Koinov, S. Konorev, V. Bondarenko, V. Yeshmyakov, and V. Schelkov. Middle row: A. Artyushchenko, P. Shabalin, A. Kalugin, and F. Ibragimov. Front row: S. Rogachev, V. Chemerilov, S. Tarasenko, and V. Povesma.

A scan of an original navigational map of Afghanistan as issued to all the VVS units deployed in the country. Notable are lines with courses and distances from different air bases. (Tom Cooper Collection)

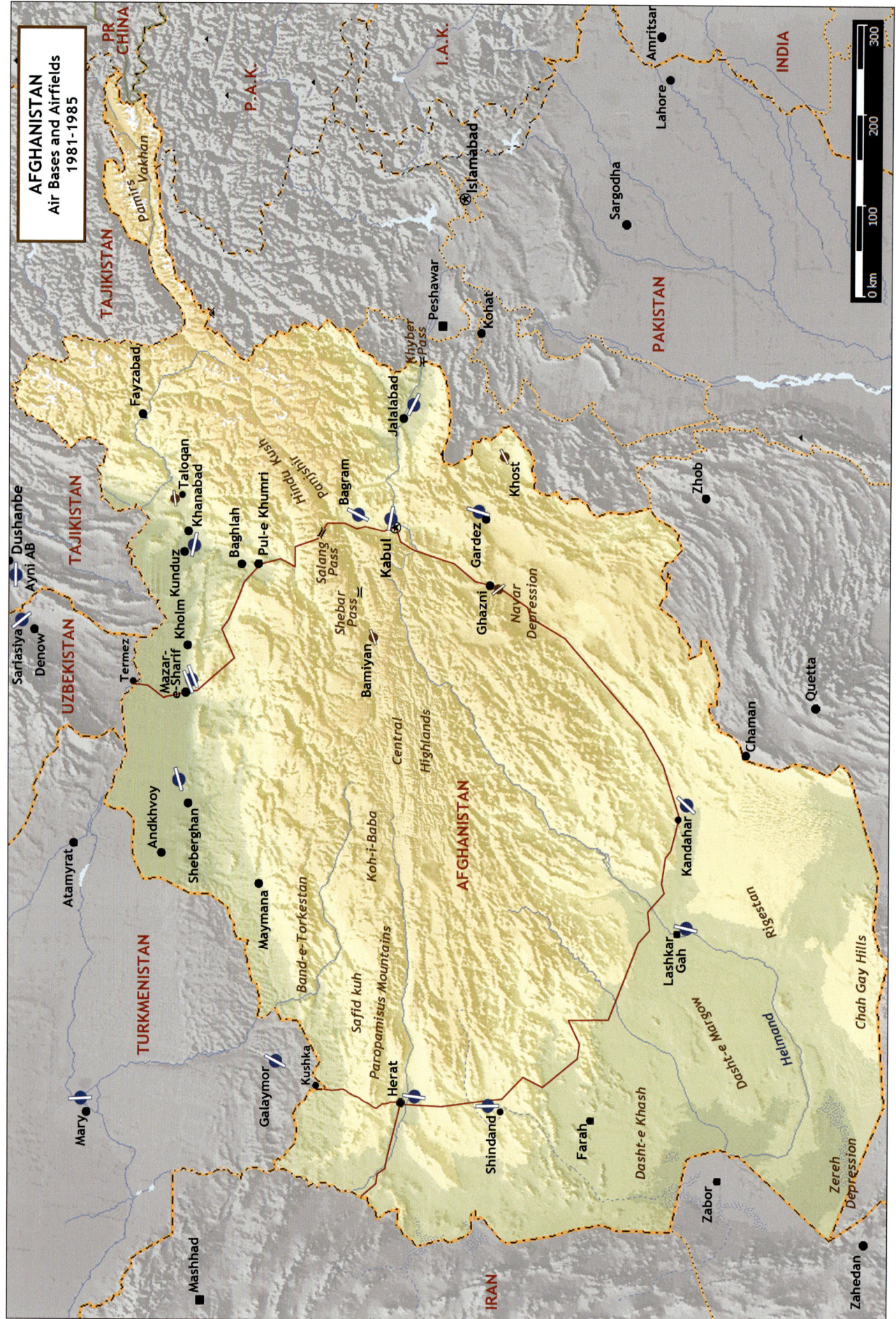

A map of Afghanistan with all air bases in service as of the 1980s. (Map by Tom Cooper)

underwent minor changes. Alexander Karpushin was appointed deputy Chief of Staff instead of Alexander Smirnov who had medical problems. The second group of retrained pilots included Ibragimov, Grushin, Butorin and Shumikhin in their shifts. In addition to conversion training, the task of raising the qualification of pilots from Class III to Class II was performed concurrently: this was in accordance with a directive of the Air Force Commander, prohibiting the deployment of pilots to the DRA with a Class lower than II.

To ensure the regiment's training in the spring of 1984, the Tarutino air training range, located 30–40km northeast of Artsiz, was established. Being much closer than the earlier range (the nearly 200-kilometres-distanced Kievo-Alexandrovskiy), this greatly increased the intensity of live firing exercises. On 10 May 1984, the regiment again flew from Artsiz to Tiraspol, where it flew very intensively. Colonel Myakenkiy and Colonel Kryachko, senior flight inspectors of the Air Force were a great asset in the training of flight personnel. These experienced officers were able to pass their vast experiences to the new generation of fliers.[2] The first commander, Nikolai Shapoalov was at least as important: he previously served on MiG-27s with the 642nd IAP at Martnovka AB. The Engineering Department was staffed by personnel from the Odessa Military District and graduates of aviation technical colleges. Since the assault regiment was being prepared for combat operations in the DRA, only those volunteering were transferred to new military unit (Military Post No. 64298) – but this proved good enough.

In April 1984, the first group of technicians – mainly people with experience on MiG-21 – left for conversion in Tbilisi at the plant named after Dimitrov. The choice of the technicians who

S. Kharchenko, first flight on the Su-25, Tiraspol, 18 August 1983.

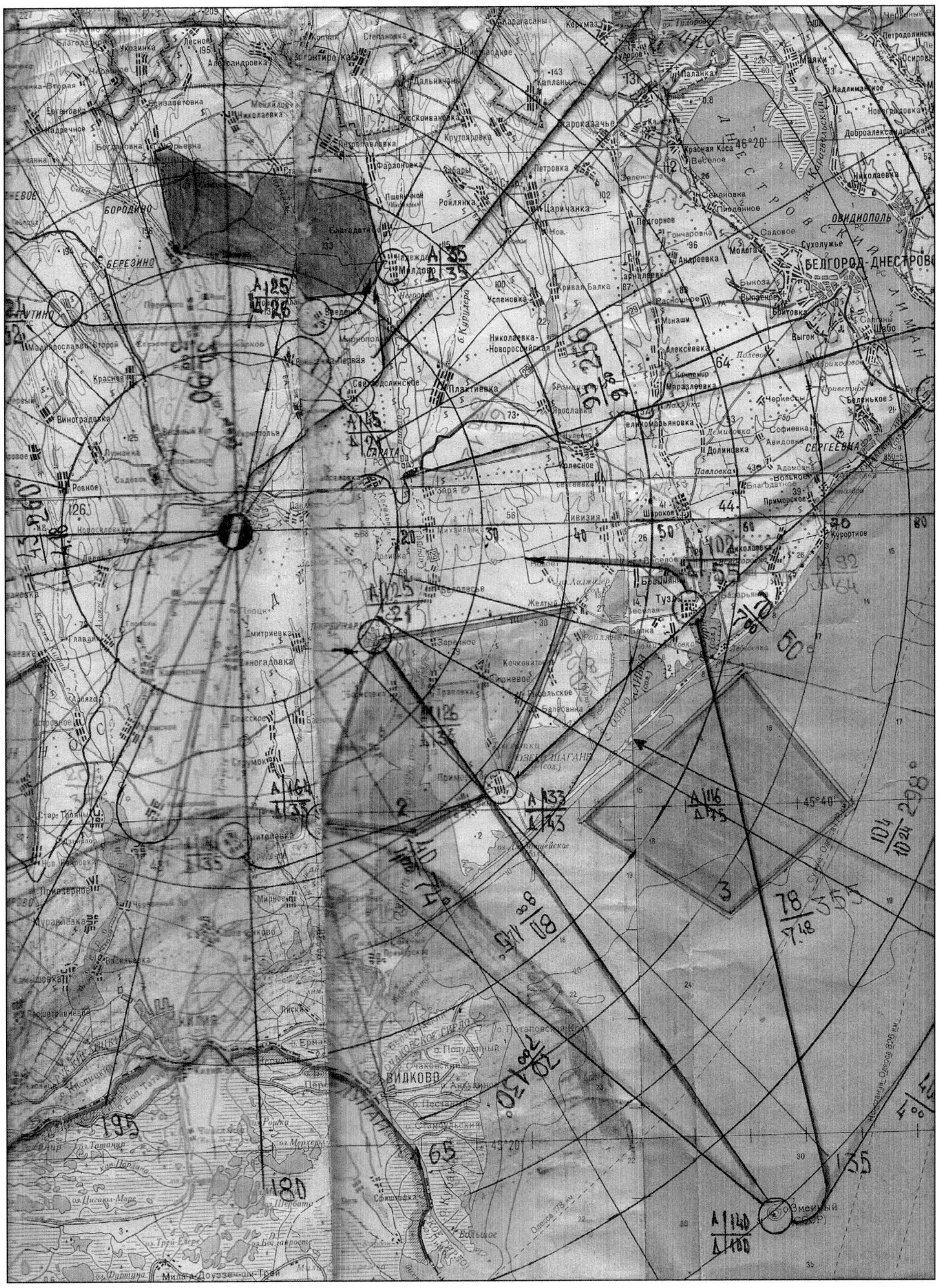

Map with the area of the airfield in Arciz and the range Tarutin.

had previously operated this type of aircraft was not accidental, since the R-95Sh engine of the Su-25 attack aircraft was, in fact, a modification of the Tumansky R-11 engine of the MiG-21. Specialists transferred from the Su-17 and MiG-27 fighter-bombers were additionally seconded to the plant in Ufa for retraining on the power plant. The training was completed by 12 May and in June, the reinforcements departed for their new duty in Tiraspol.

Off to Afghanistan

The backbone of the unit preparing for a mission to the DRA was made up of 'veterans' of the former 90th IAP, who had extensive experience in operating Su-15 type aircraft. These included the chiefs of the maintenance and repair division, Maslyakov and Silvanovich, the chief of the Airframe and Ejection Seat Department, Martsenyuk; the chief of the Locksmith, Maintenance and Repair Department, Antoshin; aircraft technicians Maslov, Kolomeitsev and others. The remaining aircraft technicians were younger: Lieutenants Uskov, Biryukov, Kravchenko, Matyushenkov, Kolosovsky, Mishin and a young Head of the Maintenance Department, Senior Lieutenant Skargin. Lieutenants Moseyev, Meledin, Sudzilovsky and Drozdov, came from Berdyansk. Lieutenants Amarfia, Bolyukh, Kertyk and Chubarev were 'guardsmen' from Markuleshti, and appointed to the vacant positions.

On 9 June 1984, at the Kiev-Alexandrovsk firing range, the squadron held a tactical training exercise, a result of which it was deemed combat-ready. Officers went on leave and on their return they performed reconditioning sorties with the main emphasis placed on training for Class II. In August 1984, training of all the junior pilots was brought to the Class II level. A few days later, the unit was ready for deployment to Afghanistan and waiting for a corresponding order at the Chirchik AB.

For the first time in the history of the 200th OShAE, a squadron other than from Sital-Chai, had been sent to replace the unit's personnel. Prior to that, only the 80th Squadron worked in Afghanistan, and then in shifts with one squadron. The relocation of the new shift from Tiraspol to Chirchik began on 3 September 1984 when the advanced team, headed by the chief pilot-inspector of the combat training department of the Air Forces of Odessa region, Colonel V. Myakenkiy and the deputy commander of the 90th Squadron, Lieutenant Colonel A. Davydov, flew to Rostov on An-12.

The next day, the second technical staff team, Su-25 attack aircraft and a pair of L-39 trainer aircraft, also flew there. The flight to the Uzbek airfield took the following route: Tiraspol – Rostov – Mozdok – Sital-Chai – Nebit-Dag – Karshi – Chirchik. Just before the departure from Tiraspol, all pilots of the squadron were met by the legendary test pilot, chief pilot of the Sukhoi Company Vladimir Sergeevich Ilyushin, who said, in the presence of the newly appointed Deputy Commander of Air Forces of the District, Yevgeny Ivanovich Shaposhnikov, the words of parting: 'Brothers! This is an aircraft-soldier! Fall in love with it, and it will not let you down!'

On 6 September, they arrived in Chirchik to meet the second group, which was scheduled to fly via the Mary-2 AB. Personnel not involved in supporting the transfer of aircraft (HQ and Technical Department) flew directly from Tiraspol to Chirchik on the IL-76 aircraft. At the local air base, the flight personnel underwent an additional training programme at the Chirchik-Gorny training range and practised a landing approach using a 'shortened pattern' with a circle altitude of 1,800m.

On 18 September, the pilots received new AKSU-74 assault rifles and ammunition and the next morning, flew to the airfield in Kakaydy where they stayed for another day awaiting the border troops from Termez. In Kakaydy, at the request of the squadron commander of the local 115th Fighter Regiment (and Shapovalov's old friend and classmate), the Su-25s received two refuelled PTB-800s and six fully-armed B-8 pods – despite the fact that the governing documents forbade flying with weaponry – and prepared the attack aircraft for take-off.

Into the Fray

On 20 September at 10:00a.m., the aircraft took off and set a course for Okab.[3] Having released the planes, the ground personnel embarked on An-12s and flew to Bagram. The squadron flew in combat formation (a pair and two flights) at ten-minute intervals. Lieutenant Colonel N.V. Shapovalov headed the group, followed by Captain S.G. Malooty. The aircraft with Bort Number 49, piloted by Senior Lieutenant A.V. Kolyako, which was flying in the second formation, crashed while landing in Bagram. The pilot was landing for the first time in an unfamiliar airfield and did not take into account the considerable landing weight, high temperature and thin air. The result of the hard landing was that the airframe of the brand new Su-25, with not even 50 hours in the air, was deformed, which led to it being written off and sent back to the Soviet Union. This left the squadron in possession of ground equipment and drop tanks (which were in high demand) marked with number 49 for the remainder of the tour.

It cannot be unequivocally judged on the commander's decision to allow the aircraft to be flown with a full combat load, in contravention of existing instructions. Knowing what risks were run by 19-year-old boys transporting fuel and ammunition for pilots along the terrible road from Hairatan to Salang to Charikar, taking 20 tons of cargo with them, was probably a justifiable risk. However, given that this was a first time for the newcomers, it would have been wiser to refrain. As for the direct 'culprit' of the incident, there was no 'administrative penalty' imposed on him. So as not to spoil the career of the young pilot, the flight incident was treated by the documents of the 40th Army Air Forces as a 'breakdown'.

Su-25 seen at high altitude during a transfer flight to Bagram with its airbrakes in open position.

Aircraft technicians V. Chubarev, A. Bolyukh, and A. Moseyev, Bagram, October 1984.

Aircraft Bort Number 48 with aircraft technician Lieutenant Mishin in the foreground, Bagram, October 1984.

Technician V. Drozdov with the Su-25 Bort Number 54, Bagram, November 1984.

Aleksandr Mikhailovich Moseyev, a Senior Lieutenant and a technician of the 200th OShAE as of 1984, recalled:

Our transfer began at 16:10hrs, on 3 September 1984, when our advance team flew from Tiraspol to Rostov-on-Don by An-12 (these words according to my notes, I was writing something down in my notebook). On 4 September we met our planes, refuelled and released them to Mozdok, where they were met by a second team. Then we were flown to Sital-Chai, from where we continued for Karshi and Chirchik (6 September), while the second team travelled via Marakh and Chirchik. The flight passed without incident. In Chirchik there was 'acclimatisation' – we got used to peculiarities of local life. The flying staff worked at the training ground. There they encountered the realities of war for the first time. They worked on the territory of the DRA from the Union, from the airfield of Kakayda. The commander of the local regiment in the Su-17 was killed. He was shot down near Salang. I learnt details later from Major Litvinyuk, officer of the helicopter regiment from Kunduz (we were in a hospital together in Kabul). Their regiment was providing search and support. The aircraft was shot down on the way out of the attack. The pilot ejected and, in the exchange of fire, was wounded first in the leg then in the abdomen near the liver. Without any ammo and seriously wounded, he hid the map and his pistol under some rocks. They were later found at the battle site. Paratroopers tried to reach him but failed: there were casualties. Judging by the damage, the pilot was killed, probably with rifle butts. Then the body was exchanged or brought back. Litvinyuk told me in detail, as he himself took part in that operation.

In Chirchik we met technicians from 200th OShAE: they were there on a business trip for a hopelessly long time, to turn in four Su-25s for repairs. The planes were from the 1st Series and in terrible condition. As I remember, this problem (handing over the old equipment) according to their words was present all the time they were in the DRA. Later, we handed over all [the] aeroplanes handed over to us, and some technicians and mechanics, I think, spent the entire Afghanistan War in Chirchik. Some even got married there!

On 19 September we flew with the advance team to Kakaidi. There we spent the night and on 20 September we sent our aircraft to Bagram. The Su-25s departed with a full load and, I think, all with six B-8 rocket launchers, to avoid burning fuel to empty and to deliver ammunition at the same time. The distance from Kakaida to Bagram was very short, so we landed in excess of the landing weight. The landing at an unfamiliar Bagram airfield was on a steep glide path – the elevation of the airfield was 1,500 metres, it was hot, the air was thin. Visibility was poor, the sun was blinding. Kolyako, onboard the Bort Number 49, failed to release brakes before levelling off, lost speed and crashed heavily overloaded on the runway. He told me this himself when I visited him in Bagram hospital where he was ill (he fell ill almost immediately – typhoid, hepatitis, a whole 'bouquet', probably due to stress and anxiety). I saw this plane later at the ramp: no visible damage but all was a bit bent. Compared to the other aircraft, all parked with their noses proudly up, its nose was down, and one wing bent. It could not be repaired, was written off and later sent off on an IL-76 to the Union, said to be in some kind of school.

And we embarked on An-12s for a flight to Bagram, at 11:10hrs, it was crowded. Thus, three of us had to take [our] place in the cockpit, three or four in the navigator's cabin, and two under in the pilots' feet. We landed at 12:50, unusually steep: the aircraft did not stop but continued rolling to a ramp between the runway and the main taxiway. We disembarked and had a look around. Bagram airfield was situated in the valley between two mountain ranges, 7km in one direction to the mountains, 12–17km in the other direction – towards the town of Charikar with its famous Charikara 'green zone'. The air base accommodated many Soviet and Afghan aircraft.

The 200th OShAE parking area was quite far away from all other aircraft parking areas, on the other side of the runway. Aircraft were housed in well-equipped stone shelters supported by earth berms, with two parking spots per shelter. There were 10 such shelters, two of which, due to some distance, were used as storage facilities (one was used to store the ground equipment). In addition to these shelters there were also aprons made of 'ironclad' material to accommodate aircraft. The single-storey squadron headquarters building was located on a small ramp between the shelters. Except for the 200th OShAE a paratrooper regiment was stationed in this area. Traces of its presence, mostly behind the shelters, were left in the form of destroyed structures, broken equipment, shell casings and miscellaneous rubbish. The squadron of our predecessors consisted of pilots and technicians from Sital-Chai. In January 1984 they lost their commander, Lieutenant Colonel Ruban. He was shot down, ejected with a roll in the gorge and hit a rock. He was flying the Bort Number 13. The shelter with the number 13 remained empty forever.

The first technician I saw, the one we were changing, looked very colourful. He was skinny, literally dried out, with his hair uncut, wearing an officer's shirt with the sleeves cut off, or rather torn off, and a pair of soldier's breeches. His technical slippers, with stomped backs on bare feet, resembled house slippers of the 'not a step back' type. He released the plane in a haze of microscopic dust that covered everything around it. This Bagram dust was as fine as powder, and omnipresent. It was everywhere! No matter how much we caulked the windows and doors in the module rooms, no matter how hard we tried to keep the rooms clean, everything was covered with a thin layer of dust. Dust hung in the air and constantly ground on our teeth. It was especially unpleasant during meals. But we quickly got used to it too. This dust also had a negative impact on the operation of machinery. Somewhere in the first stage the wing tanks did not work out. The problem was found quickly: the filters in the command pressure line of the wing tank jet pumps were clogged. The filters were removed and washed. And the dust was in the fuel. There was a problem with fuel filters in the supply battalion and the fuel in the supply tanks was not filtered. This did not happen again afterwards.

The OShAE personnel was accommodated in three modules: the flight module, the technical module and the soldier's module. In the soldier's module personnel was accommodated on one side, and non-commissioned officers on the other. There was a bathhouse next to it. Until we built our own bathhouse in the parking area, we bathed in that one. I remember a case: once after washing in the bathhouse we were sitting on a bench, waiting for the others to come out. A Mi-24 comes in and launches a rocket right above our heads. Nearby, in a couple of kilometres, there was a 'green zone' in Charik and there was someone to shoot at. I must say that by then there was constant shooting from submachine guns, machine guns, cannons and mortars in Bagram. Someone was firing all the time and the shooting increased at night. We also became accustomed to this 'front music' with time …

When our technicians arrived, there was not enough room in the technical module (after all, there were two sets of technicians) and we were placed in the soldier's barracks. In the evening we went to the technical module to get acquainted, of course with vodka. When the vodka was poured according to the traditional 'vodka-regulation norm' of half a glass we were told, 'You pour it according to the 'Soviet norm', they do not drink it like that here!' Indeed, whether it was the heat or the excess of a thousand and a half metres, the Union norm was difficult to achieve. In Bagram, plastic caps from S-5 rockets were used as drinking glasses. They were called 'nurshiki'. Vodka was poured to the lower edge of the rim. In our room of six, a bottle of vodka was enough for three toasts. The technicians, whom we were replacing, somehow immediately 'took over', i.e., they began to hand over their planes quickly, while most of the time they were lurking around dunks and cantinas,[4] selling what they had not yet had time to sell and buying up what they had not yet had time to buy. This was humanly understandable. From that moment on our 'infiltration' into the combat situation began.

Aeroplane technician Senior Lieutenant A. Moseyev.

The residential area of the Bagram AB as of the mid-1980s.

Timofey Kononenko recalled:

> By midday of the 20th our *zveno* had arrived over the Okaba circle. Malookiy's *zveno* followed shortly after us. While approaching the runway, we listened to the helicopter pilots' comments on the reaction of 'bearded' people to the 'oranges' (bombs) and 'nails' (unguided rockets) on the fly-by channel. The helicopter pilots generally communicated on a channel common to all air bases in Afghanistan and switched to the combat channel only when interacting with us. When Kolyako landed, one of helicopter pilots yelled into the radio, 'Stop landing!' We ignored this advice and landed and pulled in to the 'English' parking area. As soon as I opened the canopy, a Su-17 flew overhead from the north course at a height of 50 metres, and in the direction from where it had come, five kilometres away, a black and brown column of smoke from a burst of heavy ammunition, probably a 'five hundred', was rising into the sky. Nobody paid any attention to it, from which I deduced that it was the order of the day.
>
> We took our belongings out of the planes (it was possible to hide soldier's kit in the Su-25's cockpit), looked at the Kolyako's wrecked Su-25 and drove to the populated area. The bus we had at that time was the 'Kuban' (or the 'Kubanets', which looked like an armoured car) and Chekhov travelled in a minibus. Later, of course, Shapovalov drove it, often himself. He also gave me a ride, and once I nearly overturned. No one prepared a special meeting for us, each veteran hosted his replacement. We, of course, were given our own beds while the veterans were accommodated on cots or went to their acquaintances in the town who had vacant beds. At sunset, sitting on a long bench at the entrance to our module, we watched the Chekhov's *zveno* working in the assault 'wheel' in the area of Turn 3 (5–8km southwest of the airfield). It was very impressive. We took out a litre of vodka each (we did not take more, were afraid of customs). Actually, in the process of drinking, the transfer of battle experience began in earnest …
>
> In the morning we woke up to find the veterans gone. We had breakfast and by 08.00hrs (plus 1.5 hours to Tashkent time and minus 1.5 from Moscow time, although the longitude is practically Tashkent) we arrived at the ramp. I had a bit of a headache after yesterday. We were amazed to find out that our yesterday's party companions were getting on as if nothing had happened. Having heard a lot of 'hunting stories' on the subject, I should note that such an approach to alcohol was not the norm but, given the mode of work for months without holidays and days off, every now and then things happened …'

Captain S. Malookiy and Lieutenant Colonel V. Chergenstsov with the Su-25 Bort Number 53.

The unit quickly settled down at its new base, as recalled by T.A. Kononenko, a Senior Lieutenant in 1984:

> Preparation for the flights included study of the flight area, familiarisation with the military and political situation (composition and leadership of armed opposition units, their dislocation, armament, methods of conducting combat operations), analysis of major operations of the 40th Army for the last 6–10 months, analysis of combat and non-combat losses of the 40th Army Air Force, study of the organisation of interaction with other branches of aviation and with ground troops, organisation of search and rescue support and use of rescue equipment, then specifics of use of sighting system and weapons in the mountains. Flight maps on 1:500,000 and 1:100,000 scale were prepared for the area of operations (Panjshir Gorge, where another operation was being conducted at the time). The training sessions prior to the flights were conducted by the veterans 'on the run', so of course we received only general information on all these issues. The details were clarified in personal conversations prior to their departure. They left at the end of September on an IL-76. I remember distinctly how the 'white swan' gained altitude in a light blue sky, not colourless and burnt as in summer, and we looked at it with longing glances and thought, 'But will we live long enough to celebrate this holiday?' Not everyone lived to see it …
>
> We started flying on 23 September. The first flight was made by a standard *zveno* (Malookiy, me, Annuk, Shumikhin) to familiarise ourselves with the area of military operations. The route (approximately, the map is not at hand, and the details have been forgotten): Bagram – Surubi Reservoir – Jalalabad – Materlam – the upper reaches of Panjshir (Pasi – Shahi – Mardan), and further down the gorge to the northern extremity of Charikar 'green zone' - landing. Our formation was accompanied by a veteran who shepherded behind us and commented on the characteristic landmarks on the second frequency. The first impression of what I saw was that it was impossible to understand this chaotic jumble of mountains. But it was not. After a couple of weeks of intensive flights, the gorges, valleys and rivers shaped into a precise system

easily recognisable in details. It is difficult to explain in words, but I think, more than 20 years later, I would have easily identified my place (from the air, of course) at any point within the radius of 100–150km from Bagram. Although the mountains are visually similar, there are many small details which are typical only for this region (general direction of gorge, steepness of slopes, character of vegetation, presence of snow cover, number and mutual location of prevailing elevations, location of lateral branches from the main gorge, et cetera). A month or two later I used the 5-kilometre map of the flying area very seldom. I only needed a large scale (1km, less frequently 500m) map of the target. This map was always with me, just in case. Of course, a positive role in such an easy mastering of the flight area played was, as a rule, unrestricted visibility. With few exceptions it was from horizon to horizon. And, from a height of 10,000m to the horizon is about 350km (I calculated it myself once in Shindand, mastering a programmable calculator), and it compares with the size of Afghanistan. Of course, we did not fly at such altitudes in those days. As a rule, we flew to Panjshir at an altitude of 3,500 m (about 5,000m is standard – in the middle reaches of Panjshir Maligaram is 5,009m, we must have used it as a reference point). Towards more distant targets we gained 5,000–5,500m (along the threshold, altimetres were never reset – sometimes, when flying over the target, especially in the north, I saw altitude minus 500m on the instrument) – for reasons of fuel economy, or enemy air defences, limitations on life-support equipment (unpressurised cabin, maximum permissible altitude on Su-25 was 7,000m).

The next day, September 24, Seryoga Malooky and I went to strike at the so-called 'reserve target' in the heart of Panjshir Gorge. It was the village of Babahel, five kilometres south of the village of Pizgoran, in what we called the 'Pizgoran Cross'. The village lies in difficult terrain, on a rock ledge in a winding, narrow and deep gorge. This target was called 'reserve' because heavy military operations had already been conducted in this area for about two years. The civilian population had been long removed from there by the 'Panjshir lion', Ahmad Shah Massoud, but insurgent activity in the vicinity of the village was high. There were several such targets, which were used by the Air Force to unload before landing in case the main combat mission was impossible for whatever reason, in the vicinity of Bagram, most of them in the lower reaches of the Panjshir. Of course, there was a 'shepherd' at the back. There were no particular complaints about our work on his part. We made several bombing runs (probably four) and one or two unguided rocket firings. Later on, we went out on a couple more sorties in twos, then in a *zveno*. I remember well how we unsuccessfully bombed a fortress near Jabal Ussaraj, a settlement at the entrance to Panjshir. The 'shepherd', Chekhov's deputy Lokhov, looked and looked at this mess and then said, 'Brothers, you can't do this. Watch how you should …' and throws in a volley four ZAB-500 right in the centre of the fortress. The 'shepherds' flew their planes, we flew ours. Thus, we were put into action, the Chekhov brotherhood wished us well, and left the borders of this beautiful but miserable country.

The new shift joined in without a moment's hesitation. Having met the long-awaited replacements, the 'veterans' began to quickly hand over the planes and the remaining time was mainly devoted to resolving personal issues and preparing for their return home. Since pilots from both shifts were flying at the same time, the command of the 40th Air Army had a double set of aircraft and began to operate the equipment intensively. For most of the technicians and engineers, this was probably the most difficult period of their time in the DRA. In the Soviet Union, ammunition was quite seldom unloaded. Now they had to unload bombs, load

Senior Lieutenant T. Kononenko, Lieutenant Colonel V. Chergentsov, Captain S. Malooky, and Senior Lieutenant V. Butorin.

Senior Lieutenant T.A. Kononenko exiting the cockpit after a combat sortie, Bagram, 1985.

them onto trolleys, bring them in, hang them and load rocket units. All specialists were involved. At first, in the absence of proper experience and the necessary skill, they were very tired but gradually they got used to it and everything fell into place.

On 28 September, after the re-supply was commissioned and the logistics equipment was handed over, leaving the equipment with the replacements, Lieutenant Colonel G.A. Chekhov's squadron departed for the Union on an Il-76 and the daily routine of combat work began.[5]

The aircraft deployed to Bagram were all from the 5th and 6th production series from the Tbilisi Works and all had a guaranteed service life of 250 hours and 500 landings within two years. All had their camouflage colours applied already in the factory and they received Bort Numbers 21, 22, 23, 24, 48, 49, 51, 52, 53, and 54 in white outline only. The unit was thus two aircraft short of its authorised strength and the decision was taken to bolster it through the addition of two aircraft from the 4th series. Moreover, on 12th October, the squadron was reinforced by four newly-built Su-25s (Borts 25, 26, 27, and 28) and transferred from Chirchik AB to Bagram by pilots V. M. Annyuk, S. V. Shumikhin, V. V. Zhologov, and T. A. Kononenko. As a result, the strength in the 200th OShAE (without considering the aircraft of the previous squadron) came to 14 planes. All the attack aircraft of the 05 and 06 series were further improved in series production based on the experience gained by units in the Soviet Union and in combat use in Afghanistan. First of all, the aircraft control system was fitted with BU-45 boosters in the transverse channel, which were enthusiastically received by pilots who praised the new Rooks for their docile and easy handling. In addition, the previously established speed and maximum overload limitations were removed, gun mount assemblies were reinforced, the area of the airbrakes was increased, diverter-plates were installed on top of the airbrake nacelles and anti-glare landing lamp shields were mounted.

The 'new' unit had to fly a lot and frequently because the nine earlier aircraft were not enough to carry out the assigned missions. Virtually all the armament available on the Su-25 was used: bombs of various purposes, incendiary tanks and cluster bombs up to 500kg in calibre, KMGU containers, and S-8, S-24 and S-25 pods for unguided rockets. The aircraft were outfitted in accordance with requisitions. A typical configuration comprised two PBMs,

Chief of the Mechanical Department, Senior Lieutenant V. Kislov at the group site, Bagram, October 1984.

four 250 or 500kg bombs (OFAB – high explosive/fragmentation, FAB – high explosive, ODAB – fuel/air bomb, ZAB – incendiary, RBK – cluster munitions) and two UB-32-57 pods (containers with 32 tubes for S-5 unguided rockets with folding fins, calibre 57mm) or B-8 pods (containers for S-8 unguided rockets with folding fins, calibre 80mm). Sometimes, instead of bombs, the S-25 missiles were loaded. One pilot, Shapovalov, who usually flew the Bort Number 51, developed a strong predilection for unguided rockets. Time and again, some rockets would not go off when fired: as a rule, they were never removed, but the entire pod was re-loaded with new rockets and – during the next flight – the 'failed' rockets would launch, too.

When flying in pairs or 'on-call' missions, Su-25s were frequently loaded with six UB-32-57s, or six B-8s, or six S-24s. The internal UPU-17A cannon calibre 30mm was used frequently, especially in the early days. When the operation in the Charikar Valley was conducted, one could observe the combat application of the Rooks right from the ramp: a pair of aircraft would taxi onto the runway, take off towards Kabul and almost immediately, after the second turn, dive at the target. From the ground, one could see the bombs and rockets coming off and the guns working. Due to their use, guns were frequently dysfunctional: the third anchoring support on the barrel (in the area of the locators) was frequently breaking off. According to the manufacturer's representatives it was not recommended to use them until improvements were made, or only in emergencies. With almost a double set of planes available, the maintenance crews began to be called upon to disassemble the bombs and screw the fuses into the rocket launchers. At one moment, the most usual bombs (250 and 500kg) ran out, but large

Preparing FAB-500M-54 bombs for installation on aircraft, Bagram, 1985.

quantities of 100kg bombs were available. They were suspended manually on MBD-2-67U multiple ejector racks. Obviously, installing all of bombs on four MBDs took a long time.

In order to optimise the process of preparing the aircraft for combat sortie, the so-called 'calculation system' was applied: the technical staff of the wings prepared calculations for the time necessary for ground crews to inspect and service the jet, refuel and re-arm it. Most of the time, ground crews that were not on duty were helping out, too. In this way the time needed to prepare a unit for another flight was greatly reduced and everybody involved was less exhausted.

The squadron pilots flew in standard light blue synthetic cloth flight suits for southern latitudes. All the seats were fitted with standard NAZ-7M packs.[6] They had no time to overhaul them in the Soviet Union. Because the AKSU-74s could not fit in the cockpit, they were attached to the left side of the suspension system with the barrel up and with the horn attached. After flying so for a couple of months, Senior Lieutenant Kononenko with his warrant officer technician, contrived to cram the automatic rifle with the horn attached, but with a shorter barrel to the raft, while removing many other parts of the ejection seat except for the R-855UM radio with battery, first aid kit, morphine, and flare gun: the experience from SAR operations was that if a pilot was not onboard a helicopter in 10 to 15 minutes after an ejection, he was almost certainly dead and had no time to consume any chocolate, candies or water. In addition to the regular PM pistol (Makarov calibre 9mm) in the belt holster, pilots also carried two or three F-1 grenades in the pockets of their overalls.

Shit Happens

The intensity of combat work was taking its toll and the squadron was not without accidents. In October, while attacking a ground target, aircraft with the Bort Number 22 (construction number 25508106009, aircraft technician Lieutenant V. Matyushenko), Captain A.F. Porublev, while pressing the trigger to drop bombs, activated the jettison process for both of drop tanks and two UB-32-57 pods. The left tank then hit the nearby hardpoint and became struck: attempts to 'shake it off' proved unsuccessful. Burdened by the vertically protruding tank, the aircraft was almost uncontrollable but the pilot managed a successful emergency landing. Interestingly, on post-mission inspection, no damage was found on shackles that held the tank attached to the underwing hardpoint, nor in the electrical circuits for armament. Indeed, the aircraft was quickly returned to operations and never suffered a similar problem again: the cause for that failure was credited to 'stray currents' at the time, but actually remains unknown until today.

In the same month, when returning from another mission, the aircraft with Bort Number 24 (construction number 25508106011) crashed while piloted by Lieutenant Malyshev. He was short on fuel and announced a straight in approach but made a very hard touch-down on the runway: this caused the right landing gear to fold into the right wing and puncture the fuel tanks, while swerving the aircraft into a violent, 120-degrees turn. No fire broke out as there was no fuel in the internal tanks and the jet was handed over to the maintenance crew for inspections and possible repairs. The results of the examination were unfavourable: the airframe was severely bent and deemed non-repairable. Like in the case of the Bort Number 49, it was written off, subsequently loaded into an Il-76 transport and sent back to the USSR to serve as a training aid.

Lieutenant Malyshev was 'bent', too and grounded in punishment for this mistake. Sometime later, he fell ill with hepatitis and was then sent back to the Soviet Union, where

Captain Porublev's aircraft Bort Number 22 (pay attention at the two 'swans' on the drop tank), after landing, Bagram, October 1984. (Senior Lieutenant V. Matyushenko)

Lieutenant V. Malyshev's Aircraft No. 24 after landing, Bagram, October 1984.

Aircraft technician, Lieutenant A. Moseyev at his Su-25, Bort Number 51, Bagram, October 1984.

he subsequently served on dual-control aircraft only.

On 18 October 1984 all 13 aircraft of the 4th Series remaining were returned to the Chirchik AB in the USSR. From there, most were forwarded to the Aircraft Repair Plant No. 519 in Vaziani. Instead, a pair of Aero L-39 Albatross training jets was added to the squadron's training vehicles. Chief Warrant Officers were technicians on the Czech-made aircraft. In addition, the unit had two Su-17UM3s (Borts 80 and 88) which, together with the L-39s, were organised into a separate flight. As none of the new recruits of the 200th OShAP had experience on Su-17, they were never operated: instead, L-39s were flown whenever necessary to maintain pilot's proficiency but also for weather reconnaissance and – in the case of new pilots, or pilots who had not flown for a while – for refresher training.

Senior Lieutenant A. Moseyev with the Bort Number 24, as seen after it was raised. Bagram, October 1984.

Outcome of the Combat Work

From 27 September 1984 to 5 November 1984 the crews of the 200the OShAE of the 40th Army conducted bombing and assault flights, air support to the troops and aerial mine sowing, destroying manpower and equipment of the enemy. The personnel selflessly performed the combat missions, showing courage, heroism, high tactical skills and fidelity to the military oath.

The unit's losses during this period amounted to:

- in personnel, 0
- – in aeronautical engineering, two Su-25 aircraft were written off as a result of accidents.

Meanwhile, in October 1984 the 80th OShAE was tasked by the General Staff of the Air Force to begin to form in the DRA (and as part of the 40th Army Air Force), a two-squadron regiment based on the 200th OShAE and the headquarters section and one squadron from the 80th OShAE. Thus, came into being the 378th Independent Attack Aviation Regiment (OShAP). The 200th OShAE was disbanded on 5 November 1984 and its personnel and all equipment absorbed by the new unit.

The Su-25 Bort Number 22 in its shelter. In the stone walls the entrances to the rooms, in the background can be seen the modules of the neighbouring VDV regiment. Bagram, 1984.

CHAPTER 6
378TH INDEPENDENT ATTACK AVIATION REGIMENT, 1984-1985

The 378th Independent Attack Aviation Regiment was established officially on 5 November 1984, pursuant to the directives of the General Staff of the Air Force from 22 March 1984 and 16 August 1984, the order of the commander of the 40th Army Air Force from 27 August 1984, and the order of the commander of the 40th Army Air Force of 14 September 1984. Colonel Bakhushev took over as the commander, with Lieutenant-Colonel A. Khoyrin as Deputy Commander, Colonel U. Bardintsv as the Chief of the Political Department, and Lieutenant-Colonel V. Yakushin the Chief of Staff. The equipment of the 378th OShAP comprised aircraft from both the 80th and the 200th OShAEs, and new aircraft delivered from Tbilisi, plus two L-39 trainers.

Setting out Again

Meanwhile, early through 1984, pilots of the 80th OShAE underwent scheduled training activities. Replacements that arrived at Sital-Chai were put through their conversion training, while 'old-timers' of the regiment were enjoying breaks from flying before returning to refresh their knowledge. Essentially, the unit was preparing for another tour and intensive combat in Afghanistan. This process culminated in tactical exercises held in February 1984, during which the Su-25 was also demonstrated to an Iraqi delegation. As a result, Baghdad placed an order for 80 aircraft.

The youngest pilots of the squadron were 12 graduates of the Barnaul Military School. They concluded their conversion training at Lipetsk, in December 1983, were certified by the squadron's deputy commander, Major V.I. Romanchenko and then they began their practical training. For the latter, the unit used four Su-17UM3 of its 1st Flight, replaced by L-39s, in early 1984. At that time, the 80th OShAE was still equipped with Su-25s from the Series 1, including the Bort 71 (construction number 25508101035), which proved the most reliable example and thus, was frequently given to the novices to fly.

The lack of experience of junior officers led to several incidents. On 17 March 1984, Lieutenant P. Shabalin rolled off the runway at the end of his first solo flight. The 'culprit' later recalled:

> On March 17, I flew with Seryoga Romanov. Seryoga flew well but I had a flight accident on landing. I landed on [the] runway centerline in the middle of the landing signs, with a normal angle, but my left tyre 'found' a rebar sticking out of the concrete slab on touch-down. The wheel was 'broken' and the aircraft rolled to the left. I kept it on the runway with rudder pedals as long as the speed was sufficient for that. I released the braking chute but it didn't come out (I found out later that the pulling spring was in the wrong place). I braked, the plane flung to the right, I engaged the brakes, tried to keep the aircraft on the runway axis, but it rolled sharply to the left. With two busted tyres I slipped from the left edge of the runway into the mud at minimal speed. The nose strut broke as the Su-25 came to a halt. The commission determined the cause of the accident as the tyre failure. My fault was only in the fact that after take-off I turned off the brakes. However, I did so as instructed by the flight commander. He gave us a notebook to write down what our actions should be taken in flight.

After long and unsuccessful attempts to restore the damaged aircraft by the regiment's own efforts, it was eventually disassembled and sent to the plant in Tbilisi. There were two more cases of runway derailments in the regiment during that period, both caused by destruction of tyres due to disproportionate braking by pilots.

At the beginning of September, the squadron's tactical exercise was held. The young pilots had essentially flown the programme to be awarded a Class III flying qualification and were awaiting their well-deserved leave. However, in mid-September 1984, the 80th OShAE received an order from the commander of Air Forces of the Transcaucasian Military District to deploy with 12 aircraft to Afghanistan by 30 October. The headquarters element (six pilots from the 80th OShAE headed by Colonel Anatoliy Bakushev) and one squadron (16 pilots with squadron commander Major Anatoliy Kramarevsky) were to transfer to the 40th Army Air Force. Unknown to them, on arrival to Afghanistan, the squadron was promptly integrated into the newly-established 378th OShAP. This now had one squadron and its headquarters based at Bagram AB and another squadron – led by Major A. Kramaervsky – at Kandahar AB.

Eight pilots of Kramarevsky's squadron had flying qualification Classes I and II and had already participated in combat operations in the DRA as part of the 200th OShAE in 1982–1983. The others were new to Afghanistan and included young lieutenants, only

S. Tarasenko, A. Kalugin, A. Kramarevsky, S. Koinov with Colonel V.R. Kuzyuberdin (centre), Deputy Chief of Barnaul Higher Military School, who flew to the DRA to analyse and generalise the experience of combat use of aviation, Kandahar, 1985.

a year away from graduating as fighter jet pilots. They were equipped with brand new aircraft from the 6th Series, delivered straight from the factory in Tbilisi. However, once the 80th OShAE was subordinated to the 40th Army Air Force – and thus the Turkmenistan Military District – the command of the Transcaucasian Military District did not consider it necessary to take care to fully staff a regiment that now became 'an alien' to it. In this situation, even acquisition of the necessary office equipment fell on the shoulders of the Chief of Staff of the new regiment, Colonel Yakushin. Similarly, communication equipment was organised from the headquarters of another unit. It was thus only through several improvisations that the 378th OShAP became capable of running smooth operations in Afghanistan.

The deployment to the DRA began on 23 October 1984, when the flying staff flew from Sital-Chai to Chirchik with 12 Su-25s and two L-39s, led by two An-12s that carried the staff and ground equipment for aircraft. On the basis of analysis and generalisation of five years combat experience of Soviet aviation in Afghanistan, the command of Air Force of the Turkmenistan Military District then organised a tactical exercise that emphasised operations in mountain conditions; steep, glide-landings, flying in pairs and in *zveno* and deployment of live ammunition; but also lectures in the basic principles of Islam, in the features of life and manners of the Afghans and a number of other issues. Special attention was paid to the necessity of strict observance of personal hygiene rules and the prevention of diseases prevalent in Afghanistan (especially in form of hepatitis C).

Once preparations were ready, on 4 November 1984, the ground support equipment and some of armament were loaded into one Il-76 for transfer to Kandahar and two An-12s for a flight to Bagram. At the last minute, the order came to unload the Il-76 for the needs of a military trading company in Kabul and re-load it into two additional An-12s that arrived as replacements. Of course, somebody had to do this task and the choice fell to the pilots and technicians – who had to accomplish it manually.

On the morning of 5 November, Su-25s and L-39s escorted by two An-12s, equipment and supplies, flew to Kandahar. The third An-12 landed in Bagram. This is why 5 November 1984 also became the official day of establishment of the 378th OShAP. Initially, the total number of staff in the regiment was 30: four of them were instructors for L-39s (two in each squadron), 14 pilots were assigned to the 1st and 12 to the 2nd Squadron. The pair of Su-17UM3s left over from earlier units, were handed over to one of the neighbouring units: the 263rd Independent Tactical Reconnaissance Aviation Squadron (*otdelnaya razvedyvatelnaya aviatsionnaya eskadrilya*, ORAE)

Commander of the 1st Squadron A.A. Kramarevsky at the L-39 aircraft, Kandahar, 1985.

On the eve of the unit's departure for Afghanistan, the HQ Transcaucasian Military District reassured staff that the 40th Army Air Force was expecting the newly-established regiment to arrive and everything was in place, waiting for the troops. In reality, this was not the case: there was no housing for officers and other ranks, no buildings for regimental headquarters or maintenance facilities. Engineers were able to provide construction materials only with significant delays: the headquarters of the 378th OShAP had to organise and control the entire process of acquisition of materials and construction of necessary buildings while running combat operations.

Organising such an enterprise proved anything else than easy and required the appointment of the regimental Deputy Commander of Flight Training, Lieutenant-Colonel A.A. Khovrin to Kandahar, early on. However, already in November, eight aircraft from the 2nd Squadron were redeployed to Bagram, to reinforce the 1st Squadron. Through all of this time, junior pilots were still lacking their qualification to the Class II and thus performed no combat operations: instead, a training schedule including about 30–40 flights a month was organised for them. Thanks to the efforts of Captain V. Yehmyakov, this process was completed within two months, even though not all the pilots managed to pass the ultimate test.

A trio of Su-25s of the 378th Independent Attack Aviation Regiment as seen on the apron of Bagram AB (nearest jet wore the Bort Number 36). A MiG-21 is barely visible while taking off in the rear.

Pavel Shabalin, a Lieutenant, pilot of the 2nd Squadron, 378th OShAP, recalled:

Kandahar met us with a heat of about 30°C. We were flying away in demi-season jackets soaked through by the nocturnal 'unloading-loading' epic of the previous night. However, within – literally – 10 to15 minutes after landing, everything dried up. We helped unload everything from the two An-12s and settled into the sector previously occupied by a MiG-23 unit. Late in the evening we went to the bathhouse to meet the pilots of Su-17 and to 'pay our respects'. That was the beginning of Afghanistan for our squadron. The first time we lived in the 'fighter module': two rooms were occupied by the flight crew, two rooms were occupied by technical officers. Mechanics in the other module, the rest of the conscripts in tents. The module was actually only half-finished: we later found a way to complete it by using parts from another unfinished module. Of course, we had to carry and drag the heavy mounting plates by night and install everything by hand. That took about a month, but we were satisfied with results and began constructing a bathhouse near our module. Almost everything was ready by February or March 1985: then we received the order to relocate to Bagram, and were, once again, allocated an empty site there. The ramp was not ready, the module consisted of walls only, there were no baths or living quarters. We had to construct everything from the scratch.

In my opinion, a lot in war depends on living conditions. You need a 'corner' where you can sleep properly, where you can put your belongings (regardless how few and far between), where you can feel that this is your corner, your temporary home. In Kandahar, we 12 pilots and the squadron command lived in one room of five by three metres, where there were beds in two tiers. There was no place to hang our jackets, we walked on our legs and arms. The food situation was not good either. As a result, all these 'burdens and hardships of military service' did not fail to have an impact in the near future. In January three of us fell ill with jaundice, or rather, three of us turned in to doctors in the morning and the rest of us washed the floors with chlorine and all the signs of the same illness, because an operation was going on at Kandahar.

A view at the civilian section of the Kandahar Airport.

A bird's-eye view of Kandahar AB. Visible in the foreground are long rows of MiG-21s of the DRAAF.

Bort Number 31 of the 2nd Squadron, as seen on the finals to Kandahar, 1985.

Three jets (Borts 37, 27, and 23) of the 2nd Squadron at the apron of Kandahar, in 1985.

Bort Number 23, armed with UB-32-57 pods, as seen shortly before taxiing for take-off from Kandahar AB. Notable is the large number of very different bombs – mostly calibre 500kg – 'deposited' on their trolleys or on the ground, in the rear to the left.

Wear and Tear

The intensity of flying was very high, right from the start, and it did not take long for the aircraft of the 378th OShAE to start 'bringing home' all sorts of combat damage – ranging from hits by small arms fire, to those by DShK machine guns calibre 12.7mm and ZPUs calibre 14.5mm.

On 10 November, Su-25 construction number 25508105041, piloted by N.V. Shapovalov, sustained a 14.5mm hit that left an entry hole with a diameter of 18mm at its entry, and 50–60mm at its exit, in the rear section of the drop tank. The aircraft was repaired on the same day, in the course of four man-hours.

On 14 November, Su-25 construction number 25508106028, piloted by Capitan V.V Bondarenko, received a 12.7mm hit into the hydraulic pump installed on the wall of the 18th spar. The pilot landed safely but repairs took several weeks to complete and included not only a replacement of hydraulic pipping, but also the welding of repair sheet metal.

On 20 November 1984, Su-25 construction number 25508106014 received a 12.7mm hit into the leading edge of the right wing. The aircraft was repaired on the same day through the disassembly of the fender section and installation of sheet metal overlays.

On 24 November, Su-25 construction number 25508106013, piloted by Senior Lieutenant Yu. V. Zubkov received a 12.7mm hit in the centre section of the airframe: this left a hole of 15mm diameter and pierced a fuel tank. The ground crew replaced the fuel tank and patched up the airframe and the aircraft was back to operations by the end of the day.

The Su-25 construction number 25508105037 had the distinction of receiving damage twice during the same week. On 12 December, while flown by Lieutenant V.A. Butorin, it was hit by a 12.7mm bullet in the right inner flap section (entry hole was 15mm wide, exit hole some 20–25mm). The flap was dismantled and sheet material overlays installed to patch it up. On 16 December, while flown by Senior Lieutenant E.N. Pekshev, the same jet received a 7.62mm hit in the left stabiliser but was repaired the same day again, once again with help of sheet metal overlays.

There were also failures of equipment. A characteristic case occurred with the Su-25 Bort Number 33, taken care of by technician Sergei Gorshkov. Twice this aircraft had unpleasant

Combat damage to the drop tank of the Su-25 of 1st Squadron's Commander, Lieutenant Colonel N. Shapovalov, Bagram, 10 November 1984.

Once More into Battle

Lieutenant Colonel Alexander Antonovich Khovrin, Deputy Commander for Flight Training of the 378th OShAP in 1984, recalled:

> About the first hours and days in the Kandahar garrison.
>
> Serious attention was paid to guarding the Su-25 aircraft and all additional aviation equipment on that airfield. It took us a few days to organise accommodation and amenities for various categories of personnel. And then the air staff began to study the tactical situation in the area of military actions and the flight area itself. On 20 of November 1984, the 2nd Squadron received the first combat order to conduct aerial reconnaissance operations in pairs in the areas of the main routes of camel caravans. The attention of the 40th Army Air Forces command to the organisation of combat operations in Afghanistan, with obligatory air reconnaissance of each combat flight, was immediately evident. It was explained to us that we were in Afghanistan and not near Stalingrad: we were not pushed with our backs against the wall but were doing our international duty.
>
> Primary problem for our attacks on enemy bases was the terrain. This was like a lunar landscape, very hard to get accustomed to. Therefore, we used maps of 1:100,000 scale, so-called 'kilometre maps'. On these, we marked more or less distinctive landmarks within 15–20 kilometres from our base, laid a route to it and then approached our target from that direction. The flight back went the same way to the landmark in question.
>
> Landings in Afghanistan were unusual and consisted of a steep approach from an altitude of 2,600–3,000 metres, with engines throttle down to reduce infra-red emissions and thus the probability of being targeted by infra-red-homing MANPADS. The danger from large-calibre machine guns remained, though. On its own, this was something we [became] accustomed [to] quite easily. However, initially, everybody experienced difficulties with adjusting to strong winds that could suddenly appear, and quickly change direction. This problem was solved gradually, as we gained more experience.
>
> As of 1984, the 40th Army Air Force was already experienced in tasking its units with destruction of enemy – even in bases up to 400 kilometres away from our bases. The difficulty of accomplishing such tasks was the lack of knowledge of the local terrain, which often required Mi-8 helicopters to guide us by firing one or more rockets to indicate the target. Every such operation began by deployment of a pair of Mi-8s some 10–12km away from the target: they would go in only once we were nearby, so not to forewarn the insurgents of an impending attack.

Combat damage to the Su-25s of Lieutenant Yu. Zubkov, Bagram, 24 November 1984.

Sergey Gorshkov with his Su-25, Bagram, 1984.

surprises. When the main armament switch was turned on, bombs were spontaneously dropped on the concrete (possibly due to moisture in the armament control circuits), once while parked and the second time during taxiing. During one of the flights, after firing S-5 rockets, both UB-32-57 pods were jettisoned – as the jokers then observed, 'on the heads of the enemy'.

Problems with Ground Equipment

The greatest difficulty in operating the Su-25 in Afghanistan was preparing the aircraft for combat use, as recalled by the deputy commander of the 378th OShAP, Major V.I. Romanchenko and the regiment's Chief of Engineering Department, V.B. Kuzma. The mechanisation equipment had not been properly designed and the large number of weapons needing to be installed, caused problems. Nominally, bombs – whether calibre 250 or 500kg – would have been lifted into position with help of special trolleys with lifting trays, while smaller ones – 50 or 100kg – could be lifted on shoulders of two people. However, there were never enough trolleys with lifting trays. Therefore, heavier bombs had to be installed in the same fashion as lighter ones: they would be rolled under the aircraft on a cart, then two ordinary metal tubes were screwed in place of the fuse on either side of the bomb (front and rear). Following this, two pairs of men would hold the pipe on either side and lift it into position. The pipes would then be unscrewed and replaced by fuses. This had to be done with every single bomb, one by one. It is sufficient to say that just moving a cart with a 500kg bomb, over the uneven surface of corrugated metal, already caused huge difficulties. The carts and trolleys had wheels of such small diameter that they frequently became struck – this required the effort of several men to get them moving again. Preparing just a *zveno* of Su-25s with their maximum load of 32 bombs calibre 500kg, took as many as 48 men.

The attack aircraft were refuelled in the following way. One tanker was sufficient to service four aircraft: while ammunition was being suspended, one TZ-22 vehicle drove alongside, enabling one of the ground crew to refuel the aircraft. Usually, two aircraft – parked closely next to each other – were refuelled at the time. The vehicle then had to travel to the next revetment.

Early on, the average preparation of a single aircraft for the first combat sortie of the day, took up to 35 minutes and for the second

Senior Lieutenant A. Moseyev in front of aircraft Bort Number 27. This aircraft was lost on 10 December 1984, Bagram, December 1984.

Front view at the Bort Number 27: notable are KMGU containers suspended under hardpoints and (one) still on a trolley in front of the jet. Senior Lieutenant V. Drozdov is in the foreground, Lieutenant A. Bolyukh, aircraft technician, is on the wing (refuelling). In the background can be seen the bathhouse, still under construction (in the summer of 1985 it burnt down as a result of a rocket hit). Bagram, October 1984.

Senior Lieutenant Vladimir Ivanovich Zazdravnov, service number 16411, was born on 2 May 1960 in Moscow. He joined the armed forces of the USSR on 8 May 1977, graduated from the Armavir Military High School in 1981 and was deployed to Afghanistan starting in September 1984. He was credited with destruction of five enemy heavy machine guns and three ammunition depots. On 10 December 1984, he was credited with destruction of two DShK positions before his aircraft came under fire, the pilot lost control and hit the ground about 66km northwest of Bagram. Zazdravnov was killed. For courage and bravery, he was posthumously awarded the Order of the Red Star by the Decree of the Presidium of the Supreme Soviet of the USSR, on 28 June 1985. He was buried at Dolgoprudny cemetery in Moscow.

Senior Lieutenant V.I. Zazdravnov.

sortie, up to 1 hour and 40 minutes. Unsurprisingly, virtually the entire regiment – including pilots – were involved in the work on turning the aircraft around.

First Loss

Early December 1984 was overshadowed by the first combat loss in the regiment – and the death of pilot Senior Lieutenant Vladimir Ivanovich Zazdravnov. Lines of the combat report stated that on 10 December 1984, during the combat mission to support from the air, the actions of 682nd IAP in the Panjshir Valley, Zazdranov's aircraft was shot down and the pilot perished.

In fact, Zazdranov flew Su-25 Bort Number 27, as Number 2 in a formation led by Shapovalov on Bort Number 51. Their task was to attack insurgents in the Kidzhol area in the Panjshir Valley. Each jet made several attack runs and on the last one, they attacked with guns. While climbing from his attack, Shapovalov saw a trails of smoke rising from a gorge. Looking around, he realised he could not see his wingman. Zazdravnov also failed to reply to his radio calls. Turning around, Shapovalov continued circling around the area, all the time hoping he might see a parachute. Meanwhile, two SAR helicopters arrived, but their crew – all the time being fired upon by DShK machine guns – could not find anything. Eventually, everybody returned to base and Zazdranov was reported missing in action.

The loss of an Su-25 in combat was still a rare occurrence and thus the representatives of the Air Staff of the 40th Army quickly arrived, demanding a detailed description of the mission by Shapovalov. The first guess was that the pilot might have lost consciousness, or was injured, or even killed by an enemy bullet. Eventually, a report arrived according to which, Zazdravnov's aircraft flew into cross-fire of two DShK, one of which scored a hit on the cockpit transparency. His jet then went straight in and crashed on a mountain. A correspondingly completed report went up the chain of command and the pilot was officially declared dead: the regiment organised a farewell ceremony for him on 19 December 1984.

Zazdravnov's loss was only the third within the flying staff of the former 80th OShAE, and the jet he flew – Su-25 Bort Number 27, construction number 25508106013 – only the sixth total loss of an aircraft of this type in the Afghanistan War.[1]

Attack Methodology

The main methods of combat operations in the performance of the 378th Regiment's were predominantly strikes at predetermined targets, so-called 'planned strikes', less frequently on-call-strikes. Usually, in the evening, the regiment's command post received combat orders from the 40th Army Air Forces Headquarters for the following day, which stated approximately:

> At a distance of 5km east of the outskirts of settlement N, in a fortress measuring a × b metres, coordinates according to a Gaussian grid (specified to within 50 metres), is a squad of rebel IPA,[2] indicating field commander and number of the group. Armament (most common at the time of the conflict): RPG, ZGU-14.5, Red-Eye MANPADS, DShK, CO. 378 OShAP with six Su-25s is to strike the given target in the period (date, time with an accuracy of 5 minutes). Search and rescue support (indicate type and number of helicopters); target designation (indicate location and time). After a helicopter strike, perform photo verification of results. Interaction of strike group with SAR helicopters and targeting – on frequency …, quartz # … No civilians within R metres of target.

Often, the location of the target was indicated on a photo-planner prepared from images received from Su-17M3R reconnaissance aircraft from the 263rd ORAE or An-30 from the 50th ORAE. Usually, the regiment would receive several such orders every day. At the end of the daylight hours, the regimental commander convened the service chiefs and squadron commanders to review the orders and assess their feasibility in terms of the number of serviceable aircraft and the ammunition required to carry them out. If the requested squadron force could not be allocated, the number of crews in the groups was reduced.

The shortage of ammunition was felt quite often: at times it was necessary to use non-standard weapons; essentially, whatever was in stock. For example, heavy BetAB concrete-piercing bombs had to be used against soft targets where conventional, high explosive munitions would have been much more effective. Sometimes, the volume-detonating ODAB bombs had to be dropped, half of which failed to explode due to a lack of oxygen when the target exceeded 2,500m above sea level. Without an absolute necessity, the regimental staff tried not to use the MBD multiple ejector racks because these were causing high drag and thus a higher fuel consumption. In one case, T. Kononenko and S. Shumikhin had to make a 'straight in' landing because both aircraft were loaded with MBDs and down to 150–180kg of fuel: other jets from the same formation and not equipped with multiple ejector racks, experienced no similar problem. Moreover, as noted above, 'hanging grapes' on aircraft were extremely time-consuming and labour-intensive.[3]

Strikes were often carried out in mixed groups. For example, when handling targets in the Black Mountains, between the Surubi reservoir and Jalalabad, eight MiG-23s would strike first, followed by six Su-17, four to six Su-25s, then eight MiG-23s. Five minutes later, the first wave of Mi-8s carrying VDV troops – escorted by Mi-24s – approached from Kabul to launch a heliborne attack.

To ensure interaction between aviation and the troops in carrying out tasks of direct air support to ground troops, the 40th Army Air Forces had a special unit of forward air controllers (FACs), reporting directly to the Chief of Staff. The FAC-element on Bagram used the call sign Hussar and consisted of seven to eight men: Major V.V. Vasilyev (group commander), Captain V. Britvin, Senior Lieutenants V. Portnov and V. Tolokonnikov, Lieutenants G. Dron, A. Serbin and V. Emelyanov. Their room was in the same module as that for pilots of the 378th Regiment, however, most of the time its officers spent travelling with units in the field.

Relationships between pilots and FACs were friendly, they considered themselves a team and understood each other at a glance: the effectiveness of aviation directly depended on it. Any ground formation or unit – regiment, battalion, sometimes a company – in whose interests aviation carried out combat missions, had in its ranks, at least one forward controller. Except for air support, he was in charge of selecting landing sites and controlling Mi-8 helicopters, including evacuation of the wounded and dead. FACs received their orders from the unit commanders, in accordance with the prevailing tactical situation. They then had to assess the feasibility of the task and determine the necessary force, before forwarding the request to the flying command post (usually underway in an An-26RT, carrying the Deputy Chief of Air Staff, 40th Air Force Army). The latter would then forward the request to the command post in Bagram.

Su-25s (or Mi-24 attack helicopters) were most frequently called for so-called 'fire support'. If all Su-25s were busy or not available and the task did not involve an attack close to own troops, the mission was forwarded to units equipped with MiG-23s or Su-17s.

Obviously, this method of operations required the 378th OShAP to keep at least a pair of jets on 15 minute quick reaction alert through daylight hours, every day, every week and every month. Nevertheless, post-war statistics shows that the actual take-off usually took place within 7–10 minutes of receiving the command and that aircraft were usually over the target within 12 to 15 minutes.

War load of Su-25s for the quick reaction duty was usually as follows:

- 2 PTB-800 drop tanks on stations 3 and 9
- 2 B-8 (or, ever more seldom: UB-32-57) pods on stations 2 and 10
- 4 250 or 500kg bombs on stations 4, 5, 7, and 8.

Alternatively, six S-24B unguided rockets or six S-25O unguided rockets with high explosive fragmentation warheads and reinforced casings were suspended on stations 5 and 7 instead of bombs and rocket launchers.

When approaching the combat area, the formation leader contacted the airborne command post and the FAC, to receive the mission details. Sometimes, attacks were undertaken with help of aircraft or helicopters that acted as FAC and used pyrotechnics with coloured smoke to mark the target. However, this, rarely happened.

After checking these on the map, he would approach the target and usually, strike with S-8 rockets as first (or if the aircraft was loaded with UB-32-57 pods: with S-5 rockets). Usually, the first salvo was fired in the 'cut off' mode, during which four rockets from each pod were released: these were used to mark the target and prevent fratricide fire. Pilots would then report, 'in combat, I can see the target', then enter a dive.

In the vast majority of cases, the formation leader could not see the target during the first pass – either because it was well camouflaged or hidden inside a cave. On the contrary and more frequently, the target was identified only once the enemy opened fire. From that point on, the success of the mission depended solely on mutual understanding between the pilot and the FAC – and the spotter's capability to imagine what the pilot could see from high above, or when approaching the target at a speed of 200 metres per second, then to convey that image to the pilot in clear language (as well as pilot's capability to understand FAC's description).

The wingman usually followed the formation leader at a distance of 800–1,000 metres, observed his target, and repeated his action. It often happened that the leader's jet was taken under fire from another firing position while pulling up, then the wingman had to direct his fire at this new target. If this did not happen, the FAC spotter would clarify the position of the target relative to the leader's attack, this would then be re-attacked until the results were assessed as satisfactory. Ammunition was expended 'one at a time' (only unguided rockets were fired in salvoes of two or four for 'area targets'), requiring the aircraft to make repeated attack passes.

The Su-25-pilots considered it their duty to make as many approaches as possible and to remain in the target area for as long as possible. They understood that each additional minute of the Su-25's presence over the battlefield enabled the ground troops to raise their heads and take better positions, hence to minimise the number of combat losses. Therefore, when the bombs and missiles ran out, they put the cannon to use – and, more often than enough, the Rooks returned to base with 'dry' fuel tanks.

In the first days of large scale operations by the 378th Regiment, an 'airborne alert' was organised. For that purpose, pairs of Su-25s would be rotated continuously over the potential target zone with the next pair taking-off as soon as the proceeding was down to about 1,000kg of fuel. Early on, usual practice was for returning aircraft to 'unload' their remaining ammunition on reserve targets. However, gradually pilots began returning with their ammunition on board, even when their jets were still loaded with 1,000 and then 2,000kg – which was prohibited by the flight manual for Su-25. The reason being that everybody was aware that the ammunition was precious and it had taken a long and arduous trip from the Soviet border; additionally, its transport took lots of KAMAZ and ZIL trucks to reach them – these were protected by 18–19 year old conscripts of the Army.

Certainly enough, the ammunition was often transported to Afghanistan with help of An-12 transports. However, even for these, this was a risky mission. Moreover, the transport capacity of these aircraft was reduced to about 10,000kg because of the high altitude of air bases in Afghanistan. Finally, the pilots knew how much hard work their ground crews had to perform – usually working 20 hours a day – loading the ammunition onto their aircraft. Unsurprisingly, even the higher command turned a blind eye on such 'irregularities' like landing aircraft loaded with ammunition back to base.

Mining Operations

Except for air strikes, time and again Su-25s were deployed for visual reconnaissance – especially observation of caravan trails. Many of these resulted in strikes on detected pack animal or vehicle caravans. These tasks were performed exclusively in the 'fiefdoms' of the Mujahideen, only with the permission of the HQ 40th Air Army and after thorough coordination with its Intelligence Department. However, during the period described, such sorties were quite rare, and 'free hunting' only became widespread later.

Another task assigned to the attack aviation was to mine caravan trails, mountain passes, narrow roads and insurgent strongholds from the air using KMGU-2 containers. For such missions, the two squadrons of the 378th OShAE usually deployed two pairs of Su-25s, each loaded with four KMGUs, two PTB-800s and two B-8 pods. Several pilots were trained for this type of combat in the regiment, for example, S. Malookiy, A. Butorin, V. Zholobov, and Y. Zubkov in the 1st Squadron. The KMGU was designed for the combat use of small calibre bombs without lugs and for deployment of mines. The bomblets and mines were stowed in the container in special units and prepared for mission as follows: after opening the container hatch and locking its doors in the open position, each KMGU-2 was loaded with eight PFM-1 (so-called 'petals') or POM-1 ('oranges') anti-personnel mines. The armament specialists would set the time interval for the unloading with help of the appropriate switch, then close the hatch. Once airborne, the pilot had to press the BK SUSPENSION switch to unload the KMGU-2: explosive charges would then trigger the mines out of the container.

The Su-25 was frequently selected for the mining tasks because it was a highly manoeuvrable aircraft which could deploy mines very accurately. Also, the mining aircraft were frequently hit by ground fire whereas the Su-25's were armed and more likely to survive such attacks. Primary difficulty with deploying mines from KMGU-2 containers was that this had to be done from relatively low altitudes: not more than 400 metres above the ground. This meant that Su-25s had to fly along narrow and deep valleys, some of which were mere 2,000–2,500 metres wide. The pilot had to take care not only of his altitude but also the speed: if the jet was underway too fast, the mines were likely to be sown over a too large an area, and especially, would miss the floor of the valley; if the speed was too low, the jet might not manage to climb over the opposite slope.

When the mines fell from a height of 400 metres or more, they would burry themselves some 10–20cm deep into the soil. Their fuses were set to detonate even at slight vibrations caused by a walking man or a camel and they were lethal to about one metre around their location. To any observer on the ground and from a distance of two or three kilometres, the deployment of mines was entirely invisible – which was of importance for keeping their appearance secret.

Except for PFM-1 and POM-1 mines, the 378th OShAE sometimes made use of its general-purpose (or 'free fall') bombs calibre 100 or 260kg as mines: these then had to have their fuses set to up to 48 hours.

A definite innovation for the pilots of the 378 OShAP was the use of fuel air explosive bombs to clear Italian-made anti-personnel mines deployed by the Mujahedeen whenever they would receive

A typical, busy day at Bagram AB with most of the ground crews helping distribute 250 and 500kg bombs around different aircraft.

the intelligence about an operation of the Afghan or the Soviet Army. Such mines could not be found by mine detectors. The ODAB-500 created such a powerful shock wave that it caused mines to detonate and was thus capable of clearing large areas.

Much of what the pilots of the 378th OShAP were doing in Afghanistan was actually, 'testing' – especially in regards of how to avoid or overcome a wide range of air defence systems. All experiences were carefully recorded, studied and reviewed, time and again.[4]

Overall, the distribution of tasks in the total number of combat sorties, according to a rough estimate, was as follows:

- strikes on pre-identified targets: 55 percent
- close air support: 30 percent
- mining: 12 percent
- visual reconnaissance: 2 percent
- other: 1 percent

Pilots of the 1st Squadron: Senior Lieutenant S.V. Shumikhin, Captain V.M. Annyuk, Captain S.G. Malookiy, and Senior Lieutenant V.A.Butorin, Bagram, June 1985.

Carrying On

In December 1984, the leadership of the OKSVA and the 40th Army Air Forces Command (each of them separately), summed up the results of combat operations in 1984. For this, Colonel A.V. Bakushev, commander of the 378th OShAE and his deputies, were invited to Kabul. During these meetings many words of gratitude were expressed by multiple, top-ranking officers, including the Army commander, Lieutenant-General L.E. Generalov, the Commander in Chief of the Southern Strategic Forces, Army General Y.P. Maximov and high-ranking Air Force officers. The combined arms commanders noted the high accuracy and effectiveness of the attack aircraft and they increasingly started to favour the Su-25 for aerial support of their units.

A limited contingent of Soviet troops was fighting in Afghanistan for the sixth year. During that time, American advisers in Pakistan – having analysed Soviet air combat tactics – concluded that the reaction time of the 40th Army's command system in Afghanistan was on an order of two days. They concluded that from the moment the Air Force headquarters received information through various intelligence channels about the location of an enemy group, two days later (or a little longer) it would strike at their positions. Foreign advisers informed the leaders of the insurgent formations not to stay in one place for more than one day. This reduced the effectiveness of air strikes.

After one of the garrison meetings, the leadership of 70th Independent Guards Motorised Rifle Brigade deployed in Kandahar, suggested to the commander of the 2nd Squadron, 378th OShAP, Major Kramarevsky, there should be a closer cooperation between their units.[5] A number of issues were agreed upon, after which the squadron's Chief of Staff, Captain V.V. Bondarenko, began to receive coordinates of targets and names of settlements where squads and groups of Mujahideen were located, directly from the intelligence section of the brigade, for subsequent air strikes on them at the very last moment. The result of such close cooperation was the destruction of several large groups of enemy combatants.

January 1985 was marred by another loss. On 22 January, while returning from the battle area 12km to the north-east of Bagram airfield, the An-26RT, supporting the military operation in the Narvan Province, crashed. Aboard the plane, in addition to six crew members, were two staff officers of the 378th OShAP who directed operations of attack aviation: the regiment's senior navigator Major Viktor Stepanovich Stasiuk and deputy chief of the regiment's political department Major Alexander Alexandrovich Rudnev.

Nocturnal Operations

Until February 1985, the VVS never flew air strikes by night. Midway through that month, the headquarters of the 40th Army Air Forces ordered the 2nd Squadron to start training for nocturnal operations – foremost concentration of militants and fortified areas – with help of illumination bombs from the SAB-series. It should be noted that prior to this order, Soviet aircraft were not used in Afghanistan by night. This also prompted a change in the organisation of the squadron: Captain Romanov was transferred to the regiment's command, while Lieutenants Alkhimenko and Yakovlev were ordered to join the staff of the Artsyz squadron.

Between 8 and 10 March 1985, the regiment carried out several, high-precision nocturnal strikes against the insurgents, completely surprising them and ensuring an unimpeded advance of the ground troops. This decided the outcome of the operation conducted in the green zone of Charikar in the shortest possible time. The actions of the pilots were noted in the report of the commander of the 108th Motorised Rifle Division to the command of the 40th Army.

On 11 March 1985 the deputy commander of the second squadron, Major Zaitsev, as a result of night bombing on ground targets illuminated from the air by SABs, destroyed two jeeps which carried advisers from the USA and Saudi Arabia, plus their guards. The Chief of Staff instructed the squadron

A.A. Khovrin recalled:

In January 1985, the deputy chief navigator of the 40th Army Air Force, Colonel I.I. Timkov arrived at the airfield in Kandahar to order the 2nd Squadron, 378th Regiment, to mine main routes of mujahedin caravans from the air with anti-personnel mines. We were advised to unload in areas approximately equal to the runway (that is 50 × 2,500m). As a result, one aircraft with four KMGUs (loaded with 32 blocks, or 128 mines in total) could have mined eight sections with a total length of 20km. At 20km, the wingman would take over and perform the same task. It was obvious that applying these tactics was unexpected by the enemy and proved highly effective. Bearing this in mind, they selected minefields along the most frequently used routes of camel caravans and especially near water bodies or rivers (1–1.5km from them),[6] which were comparatively few in the desert regions of Afghanistan. Alternative targets included intersections of caravan tracks. They tried to anticipate which trails the insurgents might move on while changing their base areas, where they might end up if they used vehicles, et cetera.

For the pilot, the particularity of the mining operation was the unaccustomed duration of the KMGU's 'combat dump': about 12 seconds of horizontal flight at an altitude of 400m and a speed of 720km/h, weapons trigger pressed all the time. Eventually, eight target areas were selected and the unit accomplished the mission, although repeatedly coming under precise ground fire and while operating without any fixed objectives that could be used for orientation. Certainly enough, we had to constantly think of the enemy: where could they be hidden, where could they open fire at us? From which side they would expect aircraft to fly over? During one such bombing raid, the Su-25 of Captain V. Bondarenko was fired on from a heavy machine gun and sustained several hits. And, of course, it was saved by the fact that the aircraft had reliable armour protection covering the vital parts of the aircraft: the pilot's cockpit, aircraft engines and other units and assemblies.

One day I had a problem on my aircraft, too: when lowering the landing gear, the pressure in the hydraulic system started to drop slowly and the time it took to extend the landing gear, tripled. But the landing gear came out completely. The process of flap deployment was already in doubt as the pressure in the hydraulic system was now dropping to zero, then slowly increasing to average values. Eventually the flaps did reach the landing position, albeit over a longer period of time, but the pressure in both hydraulic systems was minimal and then dropped to zero.

This situation meant that the aircraft would have a speed of 280–290m/h after landing and there would be nothing to slow it down as the Su-25's braking system only worked if there was pressure in the hydraulic systems – which was zero at the time. The only hope of braking the aeroplane was with a brake parachute but only if there was a headwind at Kandahar airfield. A side wind would push the aircraft off the runway as there would be nothing to compensate for the drift due to the inoperative, nose wheel steering mechanism. And, if an unguided and unbraked aeroplane suddenly collides with an airfield structure, it will be impossible to avoid it as even retracting undercarriage will be impossible, again due to lack of pressure in both hydraulic systems. It remained only to watch the value of the speed of the aircraft on the runway for an inevitable collision with an airfield obstacle.

This was all my mental analysis of the landing approach situation in the air. Then I ask the air traffic control (ATC), 'What is the wind direction on landing?' He tells me that the wind at the airfield is headwind, 3–4m/sec. This is good! I did not report anything to the ATC about the failure of both hydraulic systems: he was the flight manager for the helicopter regiment and was not familiar with all the intricacies of the Su-25's design and talking to him would only have prevented me from concentrating on the essentials and acting in accordance to the prevailing situation in the air and on the ground. I landed and on the run, pulled the drogue chute at a slightly slower speed (to prevent it from breaking off as it was my only hope to stop), and it came out clearly. Everything went fine, so far. Then I switched off both engines and the aircraft's speed went down. As I moved off the runway, I dropped the braking parachute.

Eventually, I stopped after some 70 metres off the runway and while still inside my cockpit, waiting for the tractor to arrive with the aircraft's technician, an Su-17M3 was passing me, whose pilot was also in the air at the time and could not hear anything special from my radio. So he twiddles his head, 'Did I overheat if I didn't make it to my parking spot?' All I could do was to shake my hands and smile … Next, a squadron engineer, Captain N.S. Vybornov, drove up to my aircraft in a tow truck and I told him in detail about what had happened on the aircraft. Then a telegram to HQ followed and the regimental commander, Colonel A.V. Bakushev, reported to Bagram. A day later, an engineering brigade of three people from our regiment's Maintenance Department flew to the Kandahar airfield from Bagram and made my Su-25 operational again in three days of work.

commander Kramarevsky, to prepare a proposal for awarding Zaitsev the Order of the Red Banner, describing the conditions of the flight and the results of the strike (based on information from Afghan intelligence). The submission was sent to the regimental commander, Colonel A.V. Bakushev, then to the army headquarters, where it was lost.

On 14 March 1985, near the town of Talukan, the 2nd Squadron's eight Su-25s carried out a powerful attack on depots in a militant base. The timing of the attack (1 hour 30 minutes before sunset) was specifically chosen so that the aircraft approached the targets from the setting sun and thus, achieved full surprise attack. Only when making repeated bombing approaches did the enemy open fire on the planes with heavy machine guns. However, as a result of direct hits from the bombs, most of the firing points were destroyed and the attack aircraft returned to the airfield without combat damage.

Nevertheless, it was not always possible for the Su-25 to return from flights without damage. On 11 April 1985, aircraft no. 25508106026, under the command of Captain V.N. Yeshmyakov, sustained serious damage. The 12.7mm DShK bullets penetrated the armoured plate of the fuselage fuel tank and fuel pipes, causing a fire in the front section of the right wing. The pilot managed to land the aircraft but, as a result of extensive damage, the aircraft was disabled for three months.

Soon, the Army Air Staff received an order from the Army Air Forces Headquarters to deploy two squadrons at Bagram airfield from 15 April 1985. The 378 Squadron was to deploy two squadrons to the airfield, which was apparently connected with the forthcoming preparations for another large scale military operation in the Panjshir Gorge against the formations of Ahmad Shah Massoud. Earlier, the Kandahar squadron had repeatedly flown to the Bagram airbase in eights to reinforce the 1st Squadron. Lieutenants Koynov and Konorev arrived in Kandahar from Sital-Chai shortly before the relocation, and even earlier, Captain Kolyako and Senior Lieutenant Ibragimov were transferred from the 1st Squadron to the position of regimental staff. Kolyako, Koinov, and Konorev formed a truncated wing, which was jokingly referred to as 'Kuklukklansy' (the first letters of the surnames – KKK). But the personnel reshuffle did not end there. The Deputy Squadron Commander Major Zaitsev was promoted to Chief Navigator of the Regiment, Captain Yeshmyakov was appointed to his post and Captain Povesma, the leader of the second *zveno* of the squadron, was promoted to squadron commander.

The garrison was abandoned with sadness, the men not wanting to part with the (more or less) normal living conditions arranged with their own hands. During five months in Kandahar, the squadron had built a prefabricated housing unit for all categories of personnel, a permanent bathhouse made of bricks collected from the ruins of abandoned houses on the outskirts of the city – with running water and sewage disposal to the garrison sewage system, along with landscaping the area adjacent to the living area. Since the Kandahar airfield periodically came under mortar fire from the Mujahideen, to protect pilots and technicians on the ramp of the squadron, they had dug a shelter in the ground to a depth of four metres equipped with an area of 36 square metres and a metal ceiling, the top surrounded by an earth layer one and a half metres thick. In addition to providing shelter during shelling, it could also be used as a safe hiding place from the scorching heat in the summer. The camp was fenced off with a two-metre-high barbed-wire fence.

After three or four days to get settled in the new place, the flights commenced. A module was built for the pilots to live in but the parking area had not yet been prepared to receive the squadron. Aircraft and equipment were temporarily positioned near the southern end of the runway, on the ramp next to the Su-17M3R reconnaissance aircraft. The lieutenants, who had minimal flying hours during their time in Kandahar, were given

Captain V. Yeshmyakov (first from left) and pilots P. Shabalin, S. Romanov and O. Yakovlev congratulate Lieutenant Commander V. Chemerilov (second from left) on his first solo flight on the Su-25, Sital-Chai, March 1984.

a new induction programme. In the process, this was reduced. The command had faith in the young pilots who had managed to fly the entire combat area by May: Panjshir, Bamiyan, Salang, Miterlam, Surubi, south from Kabul to Ghazni, Alihail, Khost, and Jalalabad.

At the end of April, another operation, the eighth in a row, was conducted in the Panjshir Gorge against insurgent formations led by Ahmad Shah Massoud. In May, the 2nd Squadron relocated to a newly-constructed apron on the northern part of the airfield where dirt berms were built for the Su-25s, taking into account their dimensions. Once again, the attack aircraft had to settle in. During this period, a large scale military operation was conducted in the province of Kunar. Battles were fought all along the Kunar Gorge from Jalalabad to Barikot, along a frontline 170km long, with the involvement of significant forces and resources.

By early 1985, the tactical situation in the province was complex. The small garrison of Soviet forces stationed in Asadabad was opposed by a force of 6,000 Afghan Mujahedeen. To the north of Asadabad, the Soviets had virtually no control over the situation. Insurgents felt at ease there and caravans carrying arms, ammunition and reinforcements, were constantly coming from neighbouring Pakistan, with which there was a formal border. In addition, the growing strength of the enemy threatened to disrupt the road link between Jalalabad and Asadabad used for supplying troops. The reason for the beginning of fighting was the death of a Special Forces company ambushed by the Mujahideen in Marawara village, 2km northeast of Asadabad on 21 April 1985.[7] As a result, the General Staff and command of the OKSVA decided to immediately destroy the Mujahideen formations and re-open the road connecting Jalalabad with Asadabad. General V.I. Varennikov, commander of the 40th Army, and Lieutenant General I.N. Rodionov were in direct charge of the operation.

During the Kunar operation, Su-25s carried out powerful bombing and assault strikes on mujahedin positions, bases, and weapons depots set up in well-protected caves in the mountains. On the first day of an active phase of an operation, on 19 May, the aircraft Bort Number 33 (construction number 25508106030)

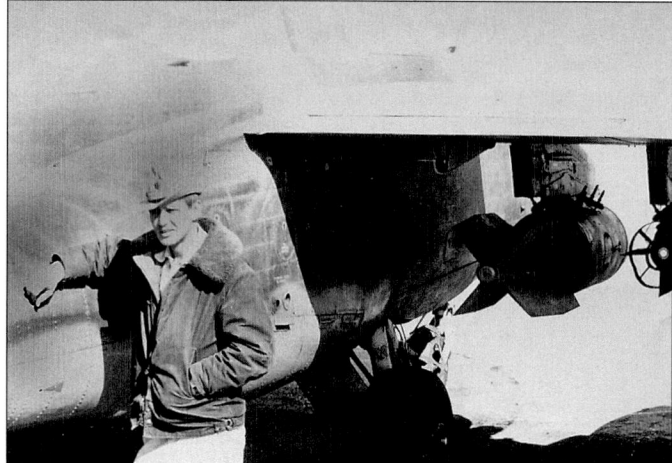

Technician S. Gorshkov, aircraft 33, at the parking lot, Kandahar, December 1984.

S. Gorshkov (right) at the training site for armament specialists, Kandahar, December 1984.

under Lieutenant P.V. Shabalin was hit by fire from a ZPU heavy machine gun. The left wing-tip was punctured near the tenth rib and in vicinity of the aileron actuator. The pilot landed without incident but the aircraft technician, S. Gorshkov, was busy for 10 hours patching up holes ranging in size between 3x4cm and 6 × 9cm.

As a result of the operation in Kunar Province, the enemy lost more than 4,200 men killed. More than 100 artillery pieces and mortars, about 200 heavy machine guns, more than 160 different warehouses, 2.5 million different rounds of ammunition and a training centre, were captured and destroyed. The decontamination of the Jalalabad-Asadabad road enabled the garrison to maintain a relatively safe supply until its withdrawal from Asadabad in the summer of 1988.

The regiment's mode of operation during large scale ground operations was as follows: rising early in the morning and working until midnight, depending on the number of combat orders and the complexity of the combat tasks assigned to them. Flight personnel and ground crews would arrive at the airfield at 03:30 in the morning. First flight would take-off at 04:30, strike at 05:00, land at 05:30. Second strike at 08:00 (breakfast from 07:00 to 09:00, which many did not get to). The third was at 11:00 (lunchtime arrival for 'leftovers'). After lunch, flight and technical staff at the airfield rested until 18:00–19:00. The tasking for the next day arranged at 11:30–00:30 at night. The pilots, in addition to the flights, helped as much as they could to bring ammunition to the aircraft in preparation for the next flight. Day after day, one could only dream of a good rest.

However, not all categories of soldiers in the regiment had such a rigid schedule. As secretary of the Komsomol organisation (youth league of the CPSU) of the first squadron, pilot P. Shabalin 'on behalf of the Komsomol of the squadron' proposed to Colonel A. Bakushev, the involvement of regiment services personnel to assist the squadron personnel during operations. The regimental commander approved this initiative with the result that both became 'enemy number one' of the 'political officers' and staff officers, who were brought in to do the heavy lifting. The conflict had a 'behind-the-scenes' continuation: the award sheet for Lieutenant P.V. Shabalin went to the bottom of the stack and Colonel A.V. Bakushev did not receive his award at all. The latter case is worth writing about separately.

The Military Council of the 40th Army decided that the 378th Regiment was worthy of being awarded the Order of the Red Banner for its combat merits. It should be noted that after the end of the Great Patriotic War, units and formations of the Air Force very rarely received awards and honorary titles (only in 1968, to celebrate the 50th anniversary of the Soviet Armed Forces). In order to be awarded, the necessary documents had to be collected in a very short period of time, the award sheet had to be filled out and forwarded to the 40th Army command. The head of the political department did not do that job and as a result, the 378th Regiment was not presented with the award. The regimental commander was in hospital with a broken leg at this time. Upon his return, A.V. Bakushev found out that the presentation had not

Lieutenant P.V. Shabalin and Senior Lieutenant F.N. Ibragimov in front of the Bort Number 30. Bagram, June 1985.

P.V. Shabalin, a participant of the Kunar operation, recalled:

> You could guess the significance and complexity of this operation from the preparations for it. We, the Su-25 pilots, were taken to Jalalabad where we met the helicopter pilots who were to take part in the operation together with us. We flew over the area of the forthcoming operation in an An-30. During this flight, fate brought me together with the commander of helicopter squadron,[8] who would later be awarded the Hero Star posthumously for this operation. He showed me the Kunar Valley through the window of the cabin and told me about it – they had flown there already. We were never prepared for an operation in this way again.
>
> In the initial phase of the operation, only experienced crews were flying and I was lucky enough to be involved from the first day until the last, although my task was very specific. My aircraft – the wing commander's, wing leader's extreme wingman – was used only for incendiary ammunition, which had accumulated in the warehouses in Bagram and Kabul. We had to use RBKs, even old RBSs from the late 1930s, incendiary bombs and napalm tanks. Anything that could burn. The experienced men did not take such ammunition seriously and it was troublesome to handle them. There was almost no reference material. I had to try everything on my own first and each individual store needed its own manoeuvre and its own special drop conditions. They started paying less attention to me and I slowly tried my own things.
>
> I was lucky enough to set fire to and destroy, an ammunition depot of the 'spirits' in the first flight of the unit. The paratroopers cheered as they watched them scatter from the target zone. From then on, I would choose my own targets in the target area while those ahead of me watched my actions and the results of my strikes. Sometimes they would adjust to me, especially when I threw incendiary canisters. The risk was very great. Apart from the fact that the tank could get stuck on the pylon during release, it could also get hit and no one could say for sure whether it would explode under the aircraft or not. In the Kunar Gorge, we had to deploy ZB-canisters against targets on slopes, at an angle of no more than five degrees to the surface. We had to fly low into the gorge, then climb slightly before deploying canisters about 200–300 metres from the peaks of surrounding hills. The whole unit worked from top to bottom: I did the opposite. After about two weeks all the incendiary ammunition ran out.
>
> I have participated in many operations in Afghanistan but the Kunar operation stands out. In terms of intensity and dedication of forces on both sides (and it was in Kunar that the 'spirits' first went into hand-to-hand combat with the paratroopers), I have nothing to compare it with. One day, I remember vividly, when almost all the staff of the regiment 'chiselled' the same height. It changed hands several times during the day. All day we worked with the FAC on their target designation, sometimes 100–150 metres from ours and actually even closer, the ammunition consisted of FAB-250s at least. All of them had one thought: whether the airborne troops would resist on this mountain or not. They held out. We then nicknamed this mountain the Sapun Hill.[9]

Lieutenant Pavel Shabalin about to sign off the aircraft preparation form, prior to the next mission. Bagram, 1985.

been sent and gave the head of the Political Department a hard time (he got as tough as hand-to-hand). As a result, the paper about the conflict went 'upstairs', but the commander was left without a personal award.

Attrition

In the summer of 1985, the Soviet government attempted to find a political solution to the Afghan problem. Mikhail Gorbachev, General Secretary of the CPSU Central Committee, instructed the Politburo to reconsider its policy towards Afghanistan. In the meantime, however, combat operations by Soviet and Afghan government forces against major armed opposition formations continued in almost all regions of the country.

The period from June to October 1985 saw a succession of near-continuous military operations conducted in Parwan, Kunduz, Helmand, Herat, Kandahar, Ghazni, Farah, Baghlan, Kapisa, Paktika and other provinces, sometimes simultaneously as three to five missions. The Rooks worked mainly 'on-call' from the position of duty at the airfield. The cockpit sometimes contained five or seven maps of different areas at the same time. There were situations when aircraft were redirected to other targets while in the air: the Su-25s would take off to the north and in the middle of the route, would turn to the south.

On 9 June, a *zveno* of Su-25s armed with S-24 rocket launchers, flew into the target area to support ground troops. On Su-25 Bort Number 35 (serial number 25508106042) the commander of the second pair, Lieutenant Colonel A.A. Kramarevsky, forgot to remove the ground safeties from his rockets. Having twice unsuccessfully attempted to fire the missiles, the pilot used a cannon on the third approach. According to the instructions, it was not allowed to use the cannon until the engine operation mode was set to low throttle: press the trigger no earlier than four seconds after setting the throttle back to 80 percent thrust. Upon firing, the engine surged and the pilot initiated the re-light procedure – without informing the ATC. On third or fourth attempt, the engine reacted: by then, he was already gliding back towards the airfield and down to less than 1,000 metres above the ground. Kramarevsky managed to land safely. Post-flight inspection revealed damage to both generators, the right engine nacelle, and to turbine blades of Stages 1, 3 and 6.

On 17 June, while performing a combat mission in a pair (Lieutenant Colonel N.V. Shapovalov and Major A.A. Karpushin), the wingman's aircraft (construction number 25508105041) was hit from ZPU into the armour plate protecting the fuel tank number two. A fire broke out in the right wing but the pilot was able to knock down the flames and accompanied by the lead, made a safe landing at Bagram airfield. The aircraft was out of service for two months undergoing repairs in the Maintenance Department of the unit. Later the aircraft was withdrawn from the service and transferred to the GNIKI for static testing.

In the period from 19 June to 30 July, during the ninth Panjshir operation, the Rooks destroyed a large number of insurgent and their ammunition depots. The actions of the pilots of the 378th OShAP were noted in the report of the commander of the 108th Motorised Rifle Division to the command of the 40th Army. On 22 July 1985, during this operation, a senior pilot of the 2nd Squadron, Senior Lieutenant Sergei Viktorovich Shumikhin, was killed in combat.

The loss occurred during a mission involving a pair of jets led by Antonuk, who flew the Bort Number 54 (construction number 25508106006). The two were attacking a set of targets for nearly half an hour. Twilight was approaching when Shumikhin, flying the Bort Number 54 (construction number 25508106006) initiated his eleventh (!) combat approach. There is no exact information about the circumstances of his loss: it is presumed that his aircraft was hit by fire from a DShK machine gun. His leader only saw Anotnuk's jet diving to attack and then hitting the ground. There was no attempt to avoid fire or climb again. This could have meant only one thing: the pilot was completely incapacitated by the hit. Sergei Shumikhin was the fourth Su-25-pilot to die in Afghanistan and his aircraft was the seventh to be written off.

On 4 August 1985, during a combat mission, the Su-25 Bort Number 34 (construction number 25508106041), piloted by the regiment's Chief of the Parachute Service, Senior Lieutenant T.A. Kononenko, sustained damage to the left air intake and an entry wound to the fuselage skin on the left side of the air intake – both from 7.62mm bullets. This caused damage to fuel tank No. 1, causing the fuel to start spilling into the engine ductwork and triggering a local combustion. Turbine blades started to melt, causing a burnout of the turbine housing, nacelle skin and tail section skin, plus melting of the wiring in the inter-motor compartment. Having received the pilot's report by radio, the control room gave an order to eject, but Timofey Kononenko put out the fire with help of the fire-extinguishing system and then made an emergency landing in Mazar-i-Sharif. The damaged aircraft landed at an airbase controlled by Afghan government troops: no Soviets were present. Soon a team from 378th Regiment was dispatched to Mazar-i-Sharif and within two days they replaced the engine and applied temporary patches to the holes, bolting them to the airframe. The pilot safely transferred the aircraft to the Bagram airfield where the aircraft was completely repaired in a matter of three days.

On 1 September 1985 the same aircraft under the command of Captain V.V. Bondarenko, during one of the attacks received numerous hits from a ZPU. The left wing and the outboard fuel tank were damaged and the aircraft was nearly out of fuel by the time it returned back to base.

After losses and battle damage, corrective action was taken. Restrictions were imposed on operating altitudes, on the maximum number of approaches and on the firing of the cannon. However, it was practically impossible to control the altitude above the target in the mountains by objective control means and the 'urgent recommendations' were soon forgotten and everything went back to normal – until the next serious combat damage. According to the recollections of the officers during this period, the atmosphere in the regiment was somewhat tense. There was some jealousy among the officers because of the special

---

Sergei V. Shumikhin

Senior Lieutenant Sergei V. Shumikhin, was born in Cheboksary, Chuvash Autonomous Soviet Socialist Republic, on 10 January 1960. He graduated from Armavir Military High School in 1982 and was deployed to Afghanistan in September 1984. He completed 244 combat missions. He displayed courage, bravery and high professionalism. On 17 July 1985, he fought against enemy air defence forces and destroyed two DShK positions. On 19 July 1985, Shumikhin personally discovered and as part of a unit, destroyed several caravans. On 20 July 1985, in the Panjshir Gorge, he discovered a warehouse with the enemy's ammunition and having overcome the air defences, dropped bombs precisely on the target. On 22 July 1985, in conditions of counteraction to air defence, Shumikhin managed to make an accurate bombing attack on a cluster of retreating enemy but the plane was shot down. Shumikhin was killed. He was awarded the Order of the Red Banner and the Order of the Red Star (posthumously). The Senior Lieutenant was buried in Armavir of the Krasnodar territory.

Senior Lieutenant S.V. Shumikhin.

attention and warm attitude to the 1st Squadron and the 40th Army Air Forces Command represented by the Deputy Commander Colonel Voronkov and the Chief of Staff Colonel Grigoruk. Perhaps this was due to the fact that members of this unit had to work very closely with the HQ 40th Army Air Force and that some of them already served with the 200th OShAE before the establishment of the 378th Regiment.

The approach to the fulfilment of the assigned tasks was also different. If N.V. Shapovalov allowed reasonable risks in carrying out the task, A.V. Bakushev prioritised flight safety and imposed restrictions on the modes of operation. However, the pilots had to spare neither themselves nor the aircraft for the quality of the bombing attack operations and had to work at low altitudes. On the other hand, knowing that the flying staff were overloaded, A. Bakushev tried to reduce the load on the personnel as much as possible. The combat orders that came to the regiment usually required a squad of forces of at least a squadron and often eight Su-25s. The regimental commander could negotiate with the command and instead of a squadron or eight, a pair would fly to the combat mission which would be just as successful in accomplishing the task at hand. Not all commanders showed such concern for their subordinates.

Tough Aeroplane

The increase in the availability of MANPADS to the insurgents resulted in growing amount of damage to all attack aircraft of the 40th Army Air Force. The low-flying Su-25s were impacted the hardest. If their engines were damaged they were simply replaced. However, there was a case where the engines had to be repaired on the spot by their own forces. For example, after one of the sorties, the aircraft was found to have warped blades of the first stage of the low-pressure compressor. With such damage, the engine should have been replaced and repaired at the factory but it unfortunately, there was nothing to replace it with at that time. Through the efforts of the regiment's technical staff, the damaged engine was dismantled and the blades were straightened then polished. The aircraft continued to fly with this engine and during the subsequent operation of the power plant, it did not cause any complaints. Another time, one of the planes 'caught a bullet' on the first

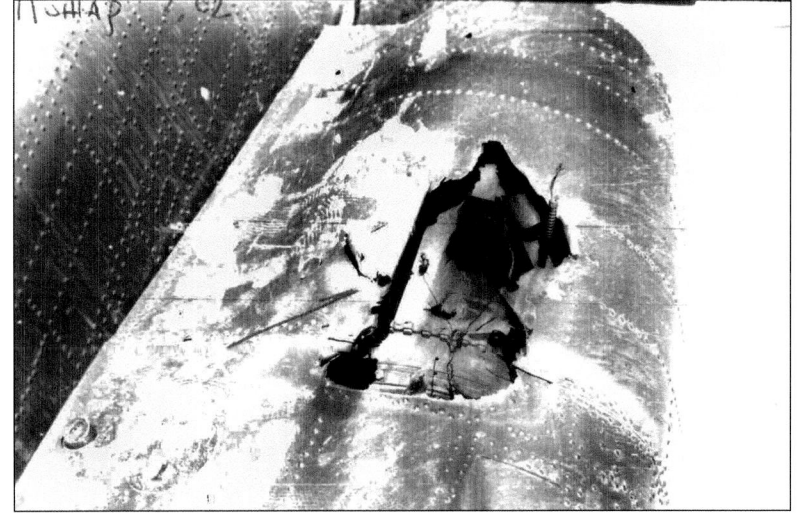

From top:
Senior Lieutenant Kononenko leaves the aircraft after an emergency landing at Mazar-e-Sharif, 4 August 1985.
Technicians working on Kononenko's Bort Number 34, at Mazar-e-Sharif, 4 August 1985.
Combat damage to the Su-25 of Senior Lieutenant T.A. Kononenko on 4 August 1985.
Repair work on aeroplane 34, Mazar-e-Sharif, 4 August 1985.

flight – the pilot did not notice it in the heat of battle and therefore, did not report it on the ground. The damage was discovered only after the fifth flight, during the routine post-flight inspection, when a technician discovered a missing blade in the turbine.

The Afghan sand was a real scourge for aircraft engines. The attack aircraft were often launched and cleared for take-off directly from dispersal sites, which reduced their preparation time for a combat flight (because the aircraft did not have to be towed to the runway). At the same time, sand was sucked into the engines through drainage holes in the metal plates of the parking area. V.B. Kuzma recalled:

An Su-25 armed with a pair of B-8 pods for S-8 unguided rockets calibre 80mm and carrying two PTB-800 drop tanks.

> Already in 1985, when I was assigned to the Airframe and Engine Department, I analysed an engine that had worked 500 hours. It had a width of the first compressor stage blade 10mm less than a new engine! The sand was 'eating away' the blade like an abrasive. When inspecting an engine that suffered combat damage, I tested it on the ground and ran a printout on the Lucha signalogram, in attempt to find out how high the temperature would get. Eventually, the first stage disintegrated and all the blades on other stages (up to the Stage 9) were battered and I could still not find out the maximum temperature. However, the engine was still running and was repairable. And that was not an isolated case: it happened on five other engines – in flight – during my tour. Such was the reliability of Su-25's engine.

An Su-25 as seen en route to the target. Notable is armament on underwing hardpoints.

The Su-25's fuel system had to be cleaned very frequently. The maintenance schedule called for the fuel filters to be cleaned every 50 hours of flight time but eventually the filters had to be cleaned every 10 hours otherwise the ubiquitous Afghan dust and sand would clog them.

The regiment continued to have a factory guarantee team working to eliminate shortcomings identified during combat operations. One day, an aircraft returned from a mission after a bombing run and the pilot reported a 40–50 metre shortfall of the bombs. The plant's sighting system specialist looked at the printout from the control system and then re-calibrated the sighting system in the usual way: by adjusting its screw by few degrees. After that everything went back to normal. The quality of aircraft assembly in Tbilisi was noticeably improved.

One claim report for a popped rivet in an aircraft under guarantee implied a 1,000 roubles fine for the manufacturer. If repair of a guaranteed aircraft due to unsatisfactory workmanship lasted more than 15 days, a penalty was imposed at the rate of 10 percent of the value of the aircraft. Therefore, cases of technical violations – like, for example, a misalignment of flying surfaces by up to three degrees (which could cause the aircraft to 'flip on its back' while manoeuvring) – all but ceased.

Overhauls in 1985

As noted earlier, in the light of experience gained in operation and combat use, the Su-25 attack aircraft were permanently upgraded both in series production and in service, according to industry bulletins. The 05 and 06 series aircraft received one more section of bimetallic and metal-ceramic discs in the wheel braking system. The brakes became more energy efficient, overheated less and there were fewer problems with fuse plugs. The fuselage design did away with all the lever locks. All nacelle hatches and cowls were fitted with key-operated 'quarter-turn' locks. The Su-25 underwent, what is known as, the second set of overhauls in 1985. Officially, no comprehensive rework was necessary but several major bulletins from the design bureau had piled up and it was decided to carry them out simultaneously. For this purpose, the manufacturer deployed a big team, well-equipped with special tools, to support of the Maintenance Department of the 378th Regiment: together, they undertook all the work directly at Bagram AB.

Changes were made to the braking parachute system: the Su-25 was initially fitted with the PTK-25 parachute-braking unit, possessing a 2 × 13 square metre white-orange, double-domed

Above and right: Su-25 in the dispersal zone of the 1st Squadron with its typical revetments. Bagram, 1985.

A Su-25 inside one of individual shelters occupied by the 1st Squadron at Bagram AB, 1985. Notable are the aircraft armament, including four bombs (inboard pylons), B-8 pods (outboard pylons) and two PTB-800 dop tanks.

parachute. This was replaced by the new PTK-25S with an increased area of 2 × 25 square metres, in green colour. The slings, halyards, draft and brake parachutes – all were made, not of aircraft silk, as the former system had, but of fibreglass which could not burn and only smouldered at high temperatures. Initially used for 50 landings, experience of operations in Afghanistan showed that it could be used for up to 100 landings. The new parachute system was intended to shorten the length of the aircraft run. However, the process of packing such parachutes was more labour-intensive and required a hydraulic press. Given that the runways at the 40th Army Air Forces' main airfields were of sufficient length, the Su-25 was also able to continue deploying the normal PTK-25 parachutes. On landing, in the presence of headwinds, they were not always released to clear the runway faster. Therefore, it was decided to use only one canopy of 25 square metre area from PTK-25S by means of minor rework. This was sufficient and in addition, the parachute resources were saved. Subsequently, this technique was also tested with regiments in the USSR.

Tough Crews

The living conditions for the technical staff were dire. Preparation for flights began at 03:00 in the morning, At the end of the combat day, post-flight preparation was carried out in the darkness with help of car headlights and torches. It was very rare for ground crews to reach their accommodation before midnight. They were only getting three, perhaps four hours of sleep per day.

In spring, the temperature at night was +4°C and during the day it sometimes reached +40°C Therefore, personnel had to go to work wearing demi-seasonal jackets in the morning and had to strip to the waist during the day. During this period, the personnel's everyday clothes (cream-coloured coveralls) were changed to experimental light green ones (not yet camouflaged). In August – September, temperatures at night and during the day were almost the same: +40°C. These months were the most dangerous in terms of infectious diseases. There were air-conditioners inside offices, but they could not cope with the summer heat. In summer, before going to bed, the technicians regularly threw a bucket of cold water over the mattress, soaked a sheet in a second bucket and quickly got into bed. It was good if one fell asleep while the bed was still wet. If not, they had to go back to get water. Some people lost up to 15 kilos of weight within two or three months during the summer period. Their rations were monotonous and poor. During the combat operations, food was brought directly to revetments. The canteen for technical staff at the airfield was a metal hangar, temperature inside of which was reaching +50°C in summer (the metal lining of the hangar heated up to 60–70°C!).

For breakfast, they were served tea and a sandwich with butter. Lunch usually consisted of borscht that was almost boiling. Alternatively, porridge and a piece of meat or a compote was served. Meat was sometimes substituted with bacon, depending on availability. The same was valid for a temporary acquisition of kangaroo meat or turkey to make stew – all of which were cooked and eaten until supplies dried up. In the evening, whoever was on duty and came to the unit before everyone else, would cook dinner – usually from canned food, cooked on an electric stove. A glass of alcohol was frequently exchanged for a loaf of bread or cabbage from the warehouse. The unit was frequently receiving extra rations of sugar, condensed milk, butter and cheese. But, in the summer, the butter was lost because of the heat: there was only one refrigerator per squadron and this were used by the pilots. In the evening after work, technicians drank 50 ml of alcohol to relieve stress and get a good night's sleep. Local water was never used as supplied, but always cooked for tea, while mineral water and juices were available in the garrison shop.

By early 1985, the 2nd Squadron had 12 attack aircraft while the 1st, had lost one. In order to replenish the strength of the 378th Regiment and because several aircraft were undergoing overhauls, they received a batch of Su-25s from the 5th Series. The four craft arrived at Bagram AB: instead of the downed Bort Number 27, there was a new one with the same Bort, thus creating a unique situation of there being three pairs of jets with the same number applied on their nose (the other were two Bort Numbers 34, construction numbers 25508106041 and 25508105032, and two Bort Numbers 25, presumably construction numbers 25508105030 and 25508106015). Additionally, between 3 and 6 October 1985, the regiment received another pair of new 7th Series aircraft, ferried from Tbilisi to Chirchik and then to Bagram. The new Su-25s had a guaranteed service life of 225 flight hours and 600 landings within two years. The assigned service life before the first medium overhaul was 800 hours and 3,000 landings over eight years. These aircraft were included in the first squadron.

Story of the Rook Insignia

In September 1985, the Rooks of the 378th OShAP received their own emblem: a year before the deployment to Afghanistan, the pilots of the 1st Squadron of the 80th OShAE were flying export Su-25Ks from Tbilisi to Czechoslovakia. While there, Vladimir Bondarenko bought a sheet of children's transferable pictures with drawings of various cartoon heroes. Already in Afghanistan, remnants of this sheet came across the eyes of Pavel Shabalin, a pilot of the 1st Squadron. Among other characters on the sheet was a raven which with a light hand of the newly minted artist, was turned into a little rook. Shabalin and Chemerilov drew the cute bird on a piece of plywood which – with the approval of Kramarevsky – was nailed to the end face of the roof of the squadron offices at Sital-Chai. However, the regiment commander did not like the drawing and several times he ordered Kramarevskiy to remove it. By then it was too late: the 'mascot' won the sympathies of pilots and even if they had to hide it from their commander's eyes, they saved it. Eventually, Kramarevsky brought it to Bagram and personally nailed it on the roof of their regimental building. Much later, the mascot was converted into an artwork applied on the Su-25s – but that is a different story.

Unauthorised symbols and images on military equipment in the Soviet Army (including aviation) were banned for decades. For many years aircraft were not allowed to bear anything other than insignia and tactical numbers. It was not until the mid-1970s, that the inscriptions 'Komsomol guarantee (quality)', 'Komsomol product name' (of a specific event or person directly related to the Komsomol organisation)', and 'Komsomol crew' began to appear. These distinctive marks on aircraft were introduced as part of the educational and Party work to raise the level of combat training in military units and were enshrined in the relevant instructions and directives of the Ministry of Defence and the Air Force Headquarters.

In order to improve the quality of aircraft operation, the honorary title 'Excellent Aircraft' was established for aircraft which had no failures during the reporting period and were maintained in exemplary order and whose crew members were excellent in combat and political training. The crew of an 'Excellent Aircraft' received a certificate and a pennant with the inscription 'Excellent' (the pennant was sewn onto the cover for the pitot tube) and on the left and right sides of the fuselage, a distinctive sign was applied representing a pentagon with an aircraft silhouette inscribed in its outline. Design bureau logos and factory emblems also began to appear on the sides of the aircraft which were applied by some manufacturing companies. It was not until the spring of 1985, to mark the 40th anniversary of Victory in the Great Patriotic War, that the aircraft were named after the heroes of the glorious units as well as those of the regiments and squadrons named after them. At the same time, Guards units were again allowed to display the 'USSR Guards' insignia on their aircraft.

Most Su-25 attack aircraft in combat units of the VVS, were like two peas in a pod. The fighting machines looked different in appearance only in their tactical numbers – which were inscribed in the factory with a thin white outline – and in the slight differences in the outline of their camouflage painting. However, the war in Afghanistan made its adjustments. Despite the fighting, the aircraft, equipment and inventory, the operational and parking areas, were kept in exemplary order. The chronic lack of free time did not prevent the encouraged aircraft technicians from inscribing on their fixed panels distinctive signs, including those of a non-regulation nature. Thus, contrary to popular opinion, the badge 'Excellent Aircraft' was affixed to the Su-25, not only in the USSR, but also in Afghanistan. At least one aircraft of 2nd Squadron of the 378th Regiment – Bort Number 21 (construction number 25508106008), was known to have received a unique, non-standard design of the badge: inscribed into the pentagon was not an abstract flying machine but the silhouette of an Su-25 ground attack aircraft.

The regiment continued the tradition of drawing stars on aircraft for combat missions. Unlike its predecessors from the 200th OShAE which applied marks on the side of the cockpit behind the Bort Number, in the 378th Regiment the place for the stars was under the solid part of the canopy. The first markings appeared on the Bort Number 22 (construction number 25508106009) in the spring of 1985. The aircraft technician Lieutenant V. Matyushenko stencilled a white star, with the number '100' inscribed in red paint. Then a second star with the number '200' also appeared. Later on, stars in white and red colour began to appear on other attack aircraft and their merit was different. Some technicians drew a star for every 100 combat sorties, others for every 50. On the same aircraft, No. 22, as early as the autumn of 1984, Senior Lieutenant A. Moseyev styled the numbers '22' on drop tanks to look like a pair of swans. Some aircraft technicians, in order to quickly identify their aircraft on the apron, also applied the digits of the flight number on the glare shield of the landing lights.

Meanwhile, the one year term of stay in Afghanistan of the first 378th Regiment was coming to an end. In October 1985, the aviators were to be replaced: under the 'Relay' programme of rotation of personnel of aviation units, a new group of pilots, ground crews and aircraft from two squadrons of the 90th OShAP was sent.

Komiska A. Kramarevsky nailing a plank with the Rook at Bagram AB, 1985.

Lieutenant S. Koynov, pilot of the 2nd Squadron, with Lieutenant Colonel V. Chergentsov, Deputy Regimental Commander and Captain S. Kovachev, Regimental Reconnaissance Commander, Bagram, September 1985.

Su-25 No. 21 with the 'Excellent Aircraft' badge from the 1st Squadron, 378th OShAE. Under the visor there are marks for combat sorties – stars of white colour. Bagram, 1985.

Outcome of the Combat Work

From 5 November 1984 to 12 October 1985, the first shift of the 378th Separate Attack Aviation Regiment of the 40th Army Air Force destroyed enemy forces, equipment of insurgents, supported the actions of ground troops on the battlefield, carried out mining of caravan tracks and trails and conducted aerial reconnaissance of the alleged locations of gangs, followed by the destruction of the detected targets.

During this period, Su-25s of the 378th OShAP flew 10,500 combat sorties and were credited with destruction of a large number of enemy manpower, arms, ammunition, 280 fortifications and 20 bases. The personnel selflessly fulfilled its internationalist tasks, displayed courage, heroism, high tactical skills and fidelity to the army oath. The reports of the commander of the 108th Motorised Rifle Division to the 40th Army Commander, dated 26 March 1985 and 15 August 1985, noted the regiment's pilots: Deputy Regiment Commander Lieutenant Colonel V. I. Chergentsov, Senior Airman Senior Lieutenant T.A. Kononenko, Squadron Commander Lieutenant Colonel N.V. Shapovalov, Deputy Squadron Commander for Political Affairs Major A.A. Karpushin, Chief of Staff, Major I. Chmil, Deputy Squadron Commander Captain A.F. Porublev, Captain B. Zholobov, *zveno*-commander Senior Pilot Captain E. Pekshev, Captain V.M. Annyuk, Senior Lieutenant S.G. Malookiy, Senior Lieutenant S.V. Shumikhin, Captain A.I. Artyushchenko and Captain V.N. Eshmyakov.

The regiment's engineering staff played an enormous role in supporting combat operations. During the period from 20 September 1984 (taking into account the work of four shifts of the 200th OShAE) to 1 January 1985, it provided a total flight time of 1,600 hours and found and eliminated, 171 defects in military equipment. The flight time per failure detected on the ground, was 11 hours, detected in the air, 62 hours and 30 minutes.

During the period of combat operations from 5 November 1984 to 12 October 1985, the regiment's combat losses were:

- in personnel, four officers, including three pilots
- in aeronautical equipment, two Su-25 aircraft

Unknown to everybody involved, thus ended only the first phase of the Rook's deployment to Afghanistan: much more was waiting for units operating the type in the coming years. Volume II will tell that part of the story.

The Rooks are going home.

Home! The squadron from Artsiz on the eve of the departure from the DRA, Bagram, 20 October 1985. Rear row: V. Butorin, E. Pekshev, V. Annuk, S. Malookiy, A. Kalita (regiment doctor) and T. Kononenko. Front row: Y. Zubkov, N. Shapovalov (Commander), B. Zholobov, N. Grushin, I. Chmil and A. Karpushin.

APPENDIX
ATTACK AVIATION AS PART OF THE 40TH ARMY AIR FORCE

Start date of combat work	End date of combat work	Dislocation	Commander	Staffing: part and dislocation
The 'Rhombus' Group				
18 April 1980	5 June 1980	Shindand	Major General Alferov V.V. (group commander) Lieutenant Colonel Vasenkov V.V. (commander ae)	MAP, GNIKI VVS
200 oshae (military unit field mail No16411)				
19 June 1981	10 September 1982	Shindand	Lieutenant Colonel Afanasiev A.M.	squadron 80 oshap, Sital-Chai
10 September 1983	26 August 1983	Shindand	Major Hanarin V.N.	squadron 80 oshap, Sital-Chai
26 August 1983	26 September 1984	Shindand Bagram: from 04.01.84	Major Ruban P.V. (died 16.01.84) Major Chekhov G.A.	squadron 80 oshap, Sital-Chai
27 September 1984	5 November 1984	Bagram	Lieutenant Colonel Shapovalov N.V.	squadron 90 oshap, Artcis
378 oshap (military unit field mail No16411)				
5 November 1984	12 October 1985	Bagram: management of the regiment, 1 ae and TECh regiment, 2 ae from 09.04.85 Kandahar: 2 ae until 09.04.85	Colonel Bakushev A.V.	200 oshae, Bagram squadron 80 oshap, Sital-Chai
12 October 1985	17 October 1986	Bagram: management of the regiment, 1 ae, 2 ae and TECh regiment Kandahar: 3 ae from 05.02.86	Lieutenant Colonel Rutskoy A.V.	90 oshap, Artcis squadron 80 oshap, Sital-Chai
24 October 1986	20 October 1987	Bagram: management of the regiment, 1 ae, 2 ae and TECh regiment Kandahar: 3 ae	Lieutenant Colonel Rutskoy A.V. Colonel Davydov (from 12.86) A. I.	368 oshap, Kalinov squadron 80 oshap, Sital-Chai squadron 80 oshap, Sital-Chai (replaced on 06.04.87)
28 October 1987	17 November 1988	Bagram: management of the regiment, 1 ae, 2 ae and TECh regiment Kandahar: 3 ae	Colonel Gonchukov G.G.	187 oshap, Chernigovka squadron 80 oshap, Sital-Chai squadron 368 oshap, Kalinov (c 21.05.88)
22 October 1988	15 February 1989	Bagram: management of the regiment, 1 ae, 2 ae and TECh regiment Kandahar, Shindand, Bagram: 3 аэ	Colonel Azarov N.I.	206 oshap, Pruzhany squadron 368 oshap, Kalinov crews 90 oshap, Artcis (c 11.1988)

NOTES

Chapter 1

1. Commission of the Presidium of the USSR Council of Ministers (CM) on Military-Industrial Issues.
2. Decree No 519-177 of the Communist Party of the Soviet Union (CPSU) Central Committee and USSR CM of 29 June 1976 on full-scale development of the Su-25 attack aircraft and setting up its serial production, was ordered for a pilot batch of 10 aircraft.
3. This date can rightly be regarded as one of the starting points in the 'new history' of domestic attack aviation.
4. Shindand was in the area of responsibility of the 5th Guards Motorised Rifle Division.
5. The Su-25 was so nicknamed because of the projecting wing leading edge and the nose section with the booms, all visible from the ground.
6. Since 1968, the airfield had been based at the 29th Separate Aviation Training Regiment of the 34th Army (Tbilisi). The regiment was training pilots for the Air Force due to staff shortages resulting from the massive downsizing of aviation by N.S. Khrushchev. They first used Il-28s and then MiG-17s from 1975 and Su-7s from 1978. In 1980, the regiment was relocated to Berdyansk and the Sital-Chai airfield emptied.
7. In the Soviet Air Force, pilots were sorted into three classes, depending on their qualifications – which in turn depended on the type of operations they were they qualified to fly. Novices began with the Class III, which envisaged only simplest combat duties by day and excellent weather. Class II envisaged more complex operations in formations larger than two aircraft, in excellent or good weather. Class I envisaged most complex operations, including by all-weather and night.
8. According to the rules for maintaining documentation adopted in the USSR (and currently Russia), the numerical designation of a military formation (subunit, unit, formation, association, et cetera) is written in Roman numerals without adding the endings -th, -i, etc, because this number is an indivisible part of its actual name, and not an ordinal number.
   For example, in the Russian documentation, correctly written unit designations are as follows:
   - 1 aviation squadron (transliteration – *1 aviatsionnaya eskadril'ya*) or one ae
   - 200 independent attack aviation squadron (*200 otdel'naya shturmovaya aviatsionnaya eskadril'ya*) or 200 oshae
   - 378 independent attack aviation regiment (*378 otdel'nyy shturmovoy aviatsionnyy polk*) or 378 oshap,
   Abbreviated designations of military formations (sub-units, units, formations) are written in uppercase, not lowercase. For example:
   - 1 ae, 200 oshae, 378 oshap, five msd (*motostrelkovaya diviziya* – motorised rifle division),
   Starting with armies, abbreviated designations are already written in uppercase letters. For example:
   - 73 VA (*73 vozdushnaya armiya*, air army)
   For the reader's easier orientation and along with Helion's house style for all @War books, these designations were adapted and transliterated, as follows:
   - 1st Squadron
   - 115th GvIAP
   - 200th Independent Attack Aviation Squadron or 200th OShAE
   - 378th Independent Attack Aviation Regiment or 378th OShAP
   - 40th Army
   - 40th Army Air Force
   - ARZ (АРЗ – авиационный ремонтный завод, *aviatsionnyy remontnyy zavod*, aircraft repair plant)
9. Organisational and staffing arrangements.

Chapter 2

1. During the Afghan war, the Panjshir Gorge was the centre of supply of arms and ammunition to anti-government forces in the northern and central parts of the country. It was the main caravan route from Pakistan to Badakhshan, Baghlan, Kapisa and Parwan provinces.
2. The Mujahideen were Islamic rebels fighting the DRA government and Soviets military forces in the country. The Soviets often referred to them as Dushman, using the Dari word for enemy or shortened to Dukh, meaning 'spirit' in Russian.
3. Boris Gromov, *The Limited Contingent* (Moscow, Russia: Progress, 1994).
4. Dimitrov Aviation Plant in Tbilisi.
5. The investigation concluded that the plane had crashed.
6. Boosters were introduced to series production beginning with aircraft no. 25508105041, while earlier ones were modified in service and at the ARZ.
7. Emergency separation system by load shedding (automatic simultaneous release).

Chapter 3

1. Korotkov, 'Monthly reports from the 40th Army Headquarters on Combat Operations in Afghanistan', *Air Combat Defence* Magazine, No. 4, 2013, p.x.
2. Slang for insurgent-controlled or dominated areas.
3. Nikolay Karev, 'Afghan Diary', www. Airforce. ru Russian Air Force: People and Planes, <http://www.airforce.ru/history/localwars/afganistan/index.htm>.
4. Frogfoot is the NATO code name for the Su-25.
5. According to France-Press.
6. Presumably the 'ill-fated' aircraft No 10 that killed the technician Akulov on shift 1.
7. The quality of aircraft assembly at the Tbilisi aircraft factory left a lot to be desired.
8. These were urgent mandatory bulletins aimed at eliminating the causes that had prompted the interruption of operations of the AT for its intended purpose (emergency works).
9. The KPM-130 is a water truck based on a ZIL-130 chassis. It is used for clearing airfields of shallow snow, sweeping, dusting, starting aircraft engines in hot weather, chassis cooling, filling objects, aircraft and vehicles with water and as a reserve fire truck.

Chapter 4

1. On command of KBP SHA and IBA – 81 for bombing and firing of APU and ANR at ground targets.
2. British 7.71mm rifle, manufactured in various modifications since 1895 under the designation 'Lee-Enfield' (Lee the name of the designer, Enfield the town where the small arms factory was located). Most probably the origin of the nickname 'Bur' came from the nickname 'Mauser', as it was used by Dutch and German settlers in South Africa, who inflicted huge losses to the expeditionary forces with their Mausers and old style 'Roer' and 'Martini' muzzleloaders.
3. Until March 1980, the 90th IAP was part of the 21st Air Division of the 8th Independent Air Defence Corps.
4. The last problem was solved in a simple way: the drop tanks were left in their place all the time, and removed only if the aircraft was to carry a full warload (for example: eight bombs or eight KMGU containers).

Chapter 5

1. A pair is a double session of two academic hours – one academic hour is 40–45 minutes).
2. Myakenkiy and Shapoalov both previously also served as a military advisers in Syria.
3. Afghan street shops and small stores.
4. Bagram airfield call sign.
5. The high results of military activity of 200 Squadron and personally its commander, Major Chekhov served as a reason for awarding him the premature military rank of Lieutenant Colonel on 18 August 1984, the day of the Soviet Air Fleet Day.

Chapter 6

1. Anton Moseyev, the technician responsible for the Su-25 Bort Number 51, painted a big heart in red on the cover of the drop tank of his jet. For this purpose, he borrowed the paint from his colleague, Andrey Bolyukh, intending to actually paint a cartoon 'ace of diamonds'. However, after the shoot down of the Bort Number 27, he stopped, and his artwork remained incomplete.
2. Islamic Party of Afghanistan. Notably, the mass of Afghan Mujahedeen was actually organised into seven different political parties, six of which (bar the one commanded by Ahmad Shah Massoud) were supported by the Afghan Bureau of the Inter-Service Intelligence (ISI) of Pakistan, on behalf of the presidency of that country. As the sole body in control of the distribution of the international aid provided from all over the World (especially by the USA and the Kingdom of Saudi Arabia), the ISI was capable of exercising at least indirect control over the activity and major operations of the military wings of the parties it was supporting.
3. 100kg bombs on multi-point ejector racks.
4. As mentioned above, the 378th OShAP was also equipped with L-39s training jets. However, these were never deployed in combat: these jets made in Czechoslovakia were used as weather scouts, radio relays, or to familiarise new pilots with the territory of operations: at least as often, they were used to provide refresher training after a leave or hospitalisation and this included live firing exercises on the firing ranges. For this purpose, L-39s could be armed with UB-16-57 pods or FAB-100bombs.
5. The 70th Brigade was deployed in the Helmland and Kandahar provinces of eastern Afghanistan and thus close to the border to Pakistan, where it saw intensive operations against the Mujahedeen. The unit was decorated with the Orders of Kutuzov and Boghdan Khmelnitsky twice.
6. Caravans would stop there to water their camels after a long crossing of the Registan Desert.
7. 1 Company of the 334th Detached Special Forces of the 15th Detached Brigade of the Special Forces of the GRU.
8. Kovalev Nikolai Ivanovich, Lieutenant Colonel, commander of a squadron of 181 Air Force ops of 40th Army, was killed on 1 June 1985. By the Decree of the USSR Supreme Soviet of 5 February 1986 he was awarded the title Hero of the Soviet Union (posthumously).
9. Soap Hill
10. The aircraft hitching hook was used with the PTK-25 and the connecting link with PTK-25C as it allowed connection of two canopies.
11. For example, the Sukhoi Design Bureau's Vityaz and Ulan-Ude Aviation Factory's logos.
12. In September 1941 the title 'Guards unit' was introduced in the Red Army. The title 'Guards' was assigned to military units, ships, formations and associations of the Soviet Armed Forces that had distinguished themselves in combat during the Great Patriotic War. The military formation received the Guards banner and personnel received the Guards title and badge. In the post-war period, the title of 'Guards' was transferred as part of continuity to preserve the combat traditions of the units distinguished in the Great Patriotic War.

BIBLIOGRPAHY

Gromov, Boris, *The Limited Contingent* (Moscow, Russia: Progress, 1994)

Karev, Nikolay, 'Afghan Diary', www. Airforce. ru Russian Air Force: People and Planes, <http://www.airforce.ru/history/localwars/afganistan/index.htm>

Korotkov, A., 'Monthly reports from the 40th Army Headquarters on Combat Operations in Afghanistan', *Air Combat Defence Magazine* (in Russian), No. 4, 2013

Extracts from the historical journals of the attack aviation regiments

Extracts from aircraft logbooks

Proceedings of the 206 shab historical museum, Lida.

'Air Force Information Digest' No. 1 (180) (Moscow, 1989)

'Flight Operations Manual for the Aviation of the Armed Forces of the USSR. NPP-78' (Moscow, 1978)

'Instruction on Aircraft Engineering Service of the Armed Forces of the USSR. (NIAS-78)' (Moscow, 1978)

V.V.Alferov, 'Serving the Fatherland. Memories of a Leading Test Engineer' (Moscow: Bedretdinov & Co. Publishing Group, 2003)

L.Antseliovich, 'Unknown Sukhoi. Years in the Secret KB' (Moscow: Yauza, Eksmo, 2008)

'Afghanistan: History, Economy, Culture' (Moscow, 1989)

'Afghanistan. Reference Map. Geographical Names Index' (Moscow: GUGK, 1982)

I.A. Bedretdinov, 'P.O. Sukhoi Su-25 and its modifications' (Moscow: R-Major, 1994)

I.A. Bedretdinov, 'The Sturmovik Su-25 and its Modifications' (Moscow: Bedretdinov & Co. Publishing Group Ltd., 2002)

E.I.Besschetnov, 'Vzletnaya strip' (Moscow: Molodaya gvardiya, 1990)

E.I. Besschetnov, 'We are Internationalists', postcard set (Moscow: Plakat, 1988)

N.Y.Vasilin, A.L.Gurinovich. 'Anti-Aircraft Missile Systems' (Minsk: Poppuri, 2002)

V.V.Gagin, 'The Air War in Afghanistan' (Voronezh: ILDVA, 2004)

B.V.Gromov, 'Limited Contingent' (Moscow: Progress, Culture, 1994)

Edited by G.F. Krivosheev, 'The veil of secrecy has been lifted. Losses of the Armed Forces of the USSR in wars, combat operations and military conflicts. Statistical Research' (Moscow: Voenizdat, 1993)

G.Yefimenko, 'Rooks. 20 Years – Flight Normal!' (Budennovsk, 2004)

'The Book of Memory of the Soviet Soldiers Who Died in Afghanistan', vol.1, A-L (Moscow: Voenizdat, 1995), vol.2, M-Y (Moscow: Voenizdat, 1999)

S. Kozlov et al, 'GRU Special Forces. Fifty Years of History, Twenty Years of War', 3rd ed. (Moscow: SPSL Russian Panorama, 2002)

S. Kozlov et al, 'GRU Spetsnaz – 2. The war is not over, the war continues' (Moscow: SPSL Russian Panorama, 2002)

G.A.Kolesnikov, A.M.Rozhkov, 'Orders and Medals of the USSR' (Minsk: Narodnaya Asveta, 1986)

A.E. Korotkov, A.Y. Kozhemyakin, 'The Su-25 Attack Aircraft. 30 years in action. Part I. In Armed Forces of the USSR 1981-1991' (Moscow, 2012)

A.A.Lyakhovsky, V.M.Zabrodin, 'Secrets of Afghan War' (Moscow: Planeta, 1991)

A.A.Lyakhovsky, 'The Tragedy and Valour of Afghanistan' (Moscow: Iskona, 1995)

V.A. Zolotarev, 'Russia (USSR) in Local Wars and Armed Conflicts in the Second Half of the 20th Century' (Moscow: Moscow, 2000)

O.S.Samoilovich, 'Near Sukhoi' (Moscow, 1999)

V.I. Feskov, K.A. Kalashnikov, and V.I. Golikov, 'The Soviet Army during the Cold War (1945-1991)' (Tomsk, 2004)

A.Sherstyuk, 'Rooks. A Quarter of a Century at War' (Budennovsk, 2009)

E. Nikitenko, 'The Afghan Campaign: Untapped Experience', Air and Space Defence Magazine, Nos. 3-6, 2008, Nos. 1-6, 2009.

E. Nikitenko, 'With Whom the 40th Army Fought. The Structure and Organisation of the Afghan Armed Opposition', Air and Space Defence Magazine, No. 2, 2010

'Afghan Insurgent Tactics', Air and Space Defence Magazine, No. 6, 2012, Nos. 2-4, 2013

'Excerpts from the 40th Army Combat Log', Air and Space Defence Magazine, No. 6, 2013, Nos. 1-2, 2014

'Monthly Reports of the Headquarters of the 40th Army on Combat Operations in Afghanistan', Air and Space Defence Magazine, Nos. 3-4, No. 6, 2010, Nos. 1-4, 2011, Nos. 1, 5, 2013, Nos. 3–5, 2014, Nos. 1-2, 2015

A. Vasilets, 'Attacking Handwriting', Krasnaya Zvezda newspaper, July 1988

V. Okulov, 'The Boy from Chkalov Street', Sobesednik newspaper, April 1988.

A. Oliynik, 'I`m Landing', Krasnaya Zvezda newspaper, December 1987

N. Kachuk, 'Sturmoviki – put on orders', Armiya magazine, No 6, 2005

A.A. Araslanov, 'Year of Life – Year of Death. Afghan diary of an assault pilot', ArtOfWar website. Creativity of veterans of recent wars, <http://artofwar.ru/a/araslanow_a_a/text_0040.shtml>

'Flight incidents in Russia, the USSR and the Russian Federation during combat operations', EVVAUL alumni forum, <http://forum.evvaul.com/index.php?topic=327.90>

A.A. Osipov, 'Lessons of the war in Afghanistan', Proza.ru website, <https://proza.ru/2014/05/20/1575>

'Fortifications of Afghan Mujahideen', Kunduz.ru website, <http://www.kunduz.ru/ukreprayony-afganskikh-modzhakhedov>

Website of Barnaul VVAUL, <http://www.vaul.ru/>
Website of Borisoglebsk VVAUL, <http://www.bvvaul.ru/>
Website of Eisk VVAUL, <http://evvaul.com/>
Website of Kachinskoe VVAUL, <http://www.kacha.ru/>
Website of Chernigov VVAUL, <http://www.chvvaul.net/>
Website of Daugavpils VVAIU, <http://www.dvvaiu.narod.ru/>
Website of Irkutsk VVAIU, <http://www.ivvaiu.ru/>
Website of Kiev VVAIU, <http://www.kvvaiu.net/>
Website of Riga VVAIU, <http://www.rvvaiu.ru/>
Website of Kaliningrad VATU, <http://kvatu.org.ru/>